STRATEGIC CONCEPTS OF GO

by
Yoshiaki Nagahara, 5-dan

in collaboration with
Richard Bozulich

THE ISHI PRESS, INC.
Tokyo, Japan

Published by The Ishi Press Inc.
Central Post Office Box 2126
Tokyo, Japan

This book and any other Ishi Press publication can be ordered from:
THE ISHI PRESS, C. P. O. Box 2126, Tokyo, Japan

First Printing February 1972
Second Printing March 1984
Third Printing November 1976
Fourth Printing September 1984
Fifth printing January 1989

ISBN 4-87187-006-5

Printed in Japan
by
SOKOSHA PRINTING CO., LTD.

CONTENTS

CONTENTS

PREFACE

The essence of Go strategy and in fact the essence of Go itself lies in the eight concepts presented in Part I of this book. An understanding of these concepts and their interrelationship is prerequisite to appreciating the beauty of Go. However, most "kyu" players are not aware of these concepts and many "dan" players have only a vague idea of their meaning. Furthermore, no one can advance to the higher "dan" levels without a clear and working understanding of these concepts. It is the purpose of this book to give the reader that understanding.

In Part I, the concepts are introduced and their relationship discussed. Part II contains problems which can be solved by utilizing the concepts presented in Part I. A serious study of these problems will in most cases result in great improvement in the skill of the reader.

This book is essentially an outgrowth of my study with Mr. Nagahara. It was written and its structure conceived by me. However, Mr. Nagahara suggested most of the examples and the others were carefully scrutinized by him.

Finally, I would like to take this opportunity to thank Mr. William Pinckard for reading and criticising the original manuscript, Mr. Stuart Horowitz for typing and proofreading the manuscript and The Nihon Kiin whose help and encouragement have made this book as well as all the other Ishi Press books possible.

Tokyo, September, 1971   Richard Bozulich

PART I

THE STRATEGIC CONCEPTS

CHAPTER 1: Miai

Miai means "seeing together". It refers to two points which are related in such a way that if one of them is occupied by a player, his opponent can handle the situation by taking the other.

Dia. 1

With 1, White plays at the central point between the two Black stones at hoshi. This creates a miai situation. That is, if Black plays tsume at 'a', White will extend to 'b', but if Black plays tsume at 'b', White will extend to 'a'. The two points, 'a' and 'b', are called "miai" because if Black occupies one of them, White must occupy the other.

Dia. 2

The sequence in this diagram is a well-known joseki. After Black 9, White can leave the situation as it is because there is no need to worry about the life of his group of four stones. Should Black attack the White group with the tsume at 'a', White can make life in the corner by playing at 'b'. On the other hand, if Black attacks from the other side by playing the osae of 'b', White can make life on the side by extending to 'a'.

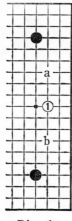

·Dia. 1

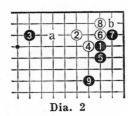

Dia. 2

An important point to notice about miai is that the two moves involved are often not urgent. That is, they are in a state of equilibrium. In Dia. 2 for example, it is not necessary for White to rush to play either 'a' or 'b' since either point will give him life. As for Black, it would be hard to decide which point to play early in the game, 'a' or 'b'. Hence, Black should defer playing either of these two points until the surrounding situation becomes more defined, allowing a rational choice to be made.

Miai is an important concept in Go strategy and functions very intimately with the other concepts, especially aji which will be introduced next. In the course of this book, many examples of miai will be encountered and its strategic significance will be more fully discussed in those places.

CHAPTER 2: Aji

Aji literally means taste; taste in the sense of food which may taste good or bad. Hence, in Go there are such expressions as "aji ga warui" (taste is bad) and "aji ga ii" (taste is good).

One of the characteristics of taste is that it lingers. It is this lingering quality which is really referred to when the word "aji" is used as a term in Go.

In Go, aji refers to a condition, whether good or bad, inherently lingering in a group of stones which offers potentialities for future play. This latent potential need not and usually should not be used immediately because this results in "aji keshi" (elimination of aji). Rather, it should be observed and studied as the game develops in surrounding areas, so that at the right time the aji can be utilized with the best effect.

In other words, aji is not a precisely defined way of playing with a fixed result, but is a future potentiality which may or may not materialize. In a sense, it is like thickness. Thickness is not territory, but it has the potential to produce territory. But, even if thickness is not realized as territory, it will have an effect on the game and, because of its presence, can cause territory to be formed elsewhere. By comparison, although the aji of a certain situation may never be realized, its existence will always have an effect on the direction of the game.

To make an analogy with war, aji is like a reserve army in the rear. Throughout the battle, even though it may never participate on the front lines, the enemy must keep considering its possible entry into the battle.

It is because of this lingering and (to one's opponent) annoying aspect that professional Go players avoid like the plague moves which result in aji keshi. The paradigm, "Don't burn your bridges behind you," can be applied to Go in the sense of leaving all possibilities (aji) open just in case they may be needed at some future time.

Dia. 1

When Black has a stone at hoshi (the star point), it is natural that he adopt a strategy which emphasizes central development. However, the placement of a stone on hoshi leaves behind the aji of an invasion at 'a' which will allow White to wrest the corner area away from Black.

Dia. 2

The sequence from White 1 to Black 12 shows one kind of joseki in which White secures life in the corner. However, Black has, as a result of this sequence, been able to form a thick wall on the outside and even though White can retain sente, the result is considered good for Black.

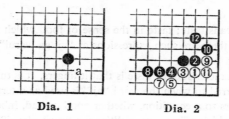

Dia. 1   Dia. 2

Dia. 3

Consider this extreme example in a six-stone handicap game. White would never want to play the sequence from 1 since the resulting Black thickness in conjunction with his stone at ● forms a much larger area than the 8 or 9 points White gains in the corner. This diagram illustrates the folly of trying to utilize aji too early in the game. In games with large handicaps, White must play more indirectly. The only times such an invasion is justified is when the resulting Black thickness will be nullified by previously played White stones or when this is the only way to reduce a large area which has already been built up.

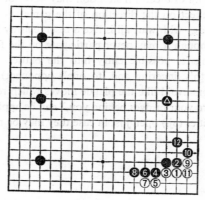

Dia. 3

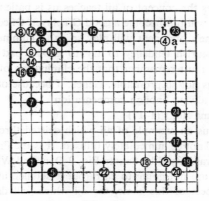

Dia. 4

Dia. 4

In this professional game, Black invades the corner at the 3–3 point. Here, this is a good strategy to adopt because no matter on which side, 'a' or 'b', White chooses to build his wall, it will be nullified by either Black 15 or 21.

Dia. 5

Diagram 5 can give us another example of aji. The point 'a' is the weak point of Black's configuration. As the situation stands now, it is impossible for White to cut at 'a'. However, if White can somehow manage to get a stone placed at 'b' or some adjacent point, the aji of a cut at 'a' will become a critical problem.

Dia. 6

This diagram illustrates why it is impossible for White to cut at 1 immediately. Even if shicho is unfavorable for Black, he can capture White with the geta of 4 and further resistance by White is useless. In evaluating this sequence, it is clear that White has allowed Black to secure at least 10 points of real profit as well as to extend his thickness farther out into the center of the board. Besides, White has lost once and for all the aji of the cut at 1. The point 'b' in Dia. 5 must be played before White can think of utilizing the aji of the point 'a'.

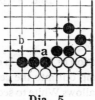

Dia. 5

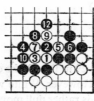

⑪ at ❷ **Dia. 6**

One of the virtues the concept of aji teaches us is patience. A person with a panicky temperament will not become a good Go player. Of course, there is always the possibility that one's opponent will play so as to eliminate his own bad aji. This causes the amateurish tendency to try to utilize bad aji too early in the game. However, one must remember that the elimination of bad aji requires an extra move and is thus not so profitable. Hence, if because of aji one can gain a tempo, this is almost always enough compensation.

Dia. 7 Illustrative Game No. 1 (1–17)

This game gives us an example of aji which existed throughout most of the middle game but could not be immediately utilized. It is the first game of the 1970 Honinbo Sen. Black was played by Sakata Eio, 9-Dan, and White by Rin Kai Ho, Honinbo Meijin. We are not going to carry out a detailed analysis but, instead, focus on only one aspect of this game, the aji which will develop on the right side. The sequence up to Black 17 completes the fuseki stage of this game and now White must consider an invasion on the upper right side of the board.

Dia. 8 (18–30)

The sequence from White 18 to White 26 is joseki. After White 28, Black attacks the White stones with 29 so as to render them eyeless, thereby making them a vulnerable target. However, White cuts with 30 and this move provides the theme for our analysis.

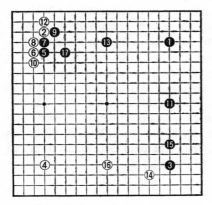

Dia. 7 (1 –17)

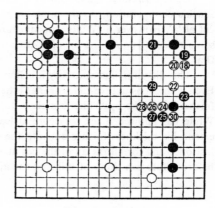

Dia. 8 (18–30)

Dia. 9

Instead of 27 and 29 in Dia. 8, the connection of Black 1 is often recommended for handicap games. However, White will jump out into the center with 2 making a good shape. Black 1 is rather dull move and allows White to secure his stones without any problems. On the other hand, this move does secure the area on the right side without leaving any bad aji.

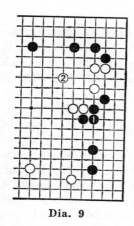

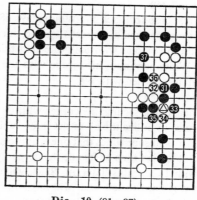

Dia. 9   Dia. 10 (31—37)

Dia. 10 (31–37)

Continuing from Dia. 8, Black settles the situation on the right side with the sequence from 31 to 35 forcing White to play 32 and 36 on the outside. After 37, even though White has managed to get his stones out into the center, they are without any eyes and will become a good target for attack in the future. However, the two White stones ◎ and 34 leave Black with bad aji on the right side and this is White's compensation for being left eyeless in the center.

Dia. 11 (38–57)

The invasion of White 38 is the correct procedure since the resulting Black thickness is nullified by the White stones on the right side. White makes life with the sequence to 56 after which Black continues his attack against the eight White stones with 57.

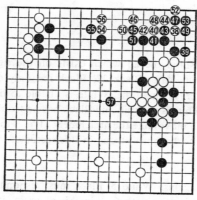

Dia. 11 (38—57)

Dia. 12 (57–69)

In response to Black 57, White plays 58 which, because of the aji of the two White stones marked ⬔, forces Black to extend to 59. Next, White plays 62 forcing Black to respond with 63. Note that this move gives White's stones an extra liberty. White continues his escape with the sequence up to 68 after which Black seals off the corner with 69.

Dia. 13

When Black secures his corner with 69 in Dia. 12 it may seem that any further chance to utilize the aji of the three White stones on the right side has become remote. It is at such times that one is apt to succumb to ones panicky temperament and feel it is high time to invade the corner. If after White 62 in Dia. 12, White invades with 1 as in this diagram, Black will exchange 2 for 3 and then play 4. Although it is hard to tell what will happen, White's stones on the upper right side seem to be in great trouble. Consequently, White 64, 66 and 68 in Dia. 12 are calm and collected moves because even though Black has played 69, the aji is still bad along the right side.

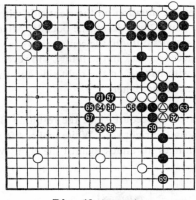

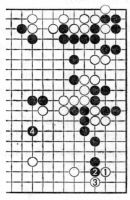

Dia. 12 (57—69)   Dia. 13

Dia. 14

In order to understand the aji which exists on the right side the sequence in this diagram is shown. After Black 22, Black has only one eye for his group along the side. However, at this time, White is unable to fight a semeai because even after 23 and 25, White is too thin and Black has no trouble gaining an eye and additional liberties with moves like the attachment at 'a'. However, if at some later stage in the game White becomes strong in this sector of the board, this aji may actually materialize.

Dia. 15

Please note that against White 5, Black must respond with 6 as in Dia. 14. If he should play osae instead with 6 as in this diagram, it will become ko with the sequence to White 11.

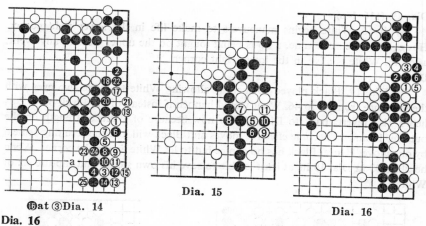

Dia. 15

⑯at ③Dia. 14

Dia. 16

Furthermore, Black cannot neglect playing 22 in Dia. 14. If he does, White can make two eyes with the sequence to 7.

Dia. 17 (70–100)

After Black ⬤, the cut of White 70 is only to be expected and the game continues along the upper side of the board. Black 99 aims at both the lower left corner and the White stones on the right side. When White defends with the kosumi of 100 it is certain that Black will begin an attack to try to kill the White stones on the right side.

Dia. 18 (101–115)

Black begins his attack with the kata-tsuki of 1. In this sequence, both Black and White made very bad mistakes (especially 108 and 109). However, we won't go into that here and we will only note that White's stones have become safe and thick in this sector of the board. As a consequence, the aji discussed in Dia. 13 now becomes a possibility.

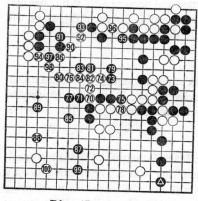

Dia. 17 (70—100)

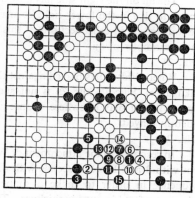

Dia. 18 (101—115)

Dia. 19 (116–146)

With 16, White begins maneuvers to make life in the lower right corner. However, at the same time, a ko is being fought on the upper side. In any event, after 46, White is alive in the lower right corner.

Dia. 20

In Dia. 19, Black played 33 thereby allowing White to make two eyes with the sequence from 40 to 46. What would happen if instead of 33, Black plays 2 as here? This reverts back to Dia. 14, but now because of White's strength on the outside, 15 and 17 become effective moves and Black will lose the resulting semeai by one move. Hence, Black has no choice but to let White live in the corner. When he plays 33 in Dia. 19 he at least is able to save his own stones and capture six of White's.

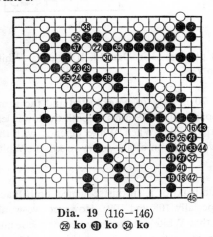

Dia. 19 (116–146)
㉘ ko ㉛ ko ㉞ ko

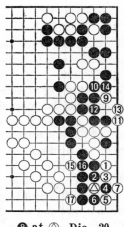

❽ at △ Dia. 20

The aji on the right side has now been settled and because of it, White has managed to live in the lower right corner. Other interesting points of this game will be touched on in other sections of this book. In the meantime, let's consider some more examples of aji.

Dia. 21

When White △ is played against the Black stone marked ▲, it is called niken-takagakari. Since White △ is not such a severe attack, Black often chooses to ignore it and play elsewhere. Consequently, the attachment of White 1 is frequently played.

Dia. 22

In response to the attachment of White 1, Black 2 is natural. White must cross-cut with 3 and Black descends with 4. Commencing with 5, White embarks on a sequence in order to make a shape which will create aji in the corner allowing him to perfect his outside thickness. The tsuke of Black 6 is tesuji and White makes

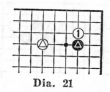

Dia. 21

Dia. 22

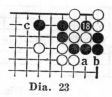

Dia. 23

his desired shape with the sequence up to 11. Black 12 is now necessary, after which White makes shape in the center with 13. Next, Black must go back and capture the White stones in the corner while White plays shibori with 15 and takes two Black stones with 17.

Dia. 23

Finally, Black plays 18 and this joseki comes to a close. At first glance, it may seem that Black's profit is much better than White's outside thickness, but on closer inspection it will be seen that the aji of the six White stones in the corner has considerable effect. First of all there is the shibori of White 'a' and 'b'. In addition, it is also possible for White to make a wall along the upper side with the tsuke of 'c'. However, this tsuke depends on the presence of the six White stones in the corner. Therefore, White must not play at 'a' and 'b' too soon as it would erase the aji of the tsuke at 'c'. Let's examine this aji in more detail.

Dia. 24

If White finds it advantageous to seal off the upper side (either to make territory or, perhaps, to kill a group of Black stones), he can attach with 1. Of course, if Black is really intent on preventing this blockade, he can play 2, 4 and 6. But now the aji of the six "dead" White stones makes itself felt and White is able to save these stones as well as to take the upper right corner territory.

Dia. 25

For Black to give up the corner as in Dia. 24 is a very big loss. Hence, Black will most likely play 2. Next, White plays 3, sealing off the upper side. However, Black is now able to play at 'a' and invade the right side.

In the early stages of the game when this joseki would probably be played, it is impossible to tell on which side White will want to make thickness. If he seals off one side, he loses the option of sealing off the other side. Consequently, for White to either play 'a' and 'b', or to play 'c' in Dia. 23 too soon would be aji keshi.

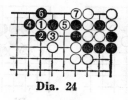

Dia. 24

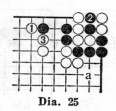

Dia. 25

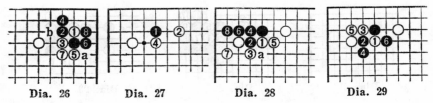

| Dia. 26 | Dia. 27 | Dia. 28 | Dia. 29 |

Dia. 26

In order to emphasize the value of the aji of the sacrificed stones in the joseki of Dia. 21, consider the situation if this sacrifice is not made. In response to the sagari of Black 4, White simply plays 5 and connects with 7. Of course, Black must play 8 allowing White to retain sente, but now there is no aji in the corner. If White plays either 'a' or 'b', these moves will have no effect on the life or death of the corner and so Black can play elsewhere.

Dia. 27

Let us consider another situation. When White plays ikken-basami with 2, it sometimes happens that Black will not respond but play elsewhere on the board. In such a case, White 4 is a natural continuation.

Dia. 28

In response to White 1, the hanekomi of Black 2 is joseki and the sequence continues to Black 8, White obtaining outside thickness and Black taking the corner.

Dia. 29 Shicho

However when Black plays the hanekomi of 2, there is a shicho relation which must be considered. Suppose White plays ate with 3 from below. The sequence to Black 6 results in shicho and if it is unfavorable for Black, the result will be a disaster for him.

Dia. 30 Sente

It will be noticed that Dia. 28 ends in gote for Black. The reader might ask, "Doesn't Black 8 in this diagram allow Black to come away from the encounter with sente?" The answer is "yes," but this 8 is aji keshi and now Black is no longer able to cut at 'a'.

Dia. 31 Black lives

If White plays 1 and 3, Black can live with 2 and 4, but, now 'a' is a big yose point against which Black must respond and his profit in the corner has become negligible.

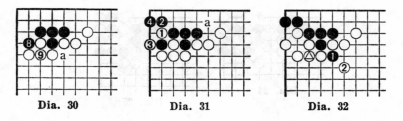

| Dia. 30 | Dia. 31 | Dia. 32 |

Dia. 32 Geta

In addition, if Black cuts at 1, because of the presence of White ⊘, caused by Black 8 in Dia. 30, White can capture this stone with the geta of 2.

Consequently, Black 8 in Dia. 30 cannot be recommended. It is more reasonable to play 8 as in Dia. 28 even though this ends in gote. Not only does it leave the aji at 'a' in Dia. 28, but the profit in the corner is larger. The value of this aji must not be underestimated. Furthermore, to play 8 in gote is not so unbearable as it must be remembered that Black has already played tenuki once in this corner when he originally neglected to answer the hasami of White 2 in Dia. 27. Therefore, it is more valuable to live in the corner, patiently waiting for a chance to utilize the aji at 'a' in Dia. 28.

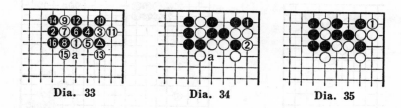

Dia. 33　　　　　　Dia. 34　　　　　　Dia. 35

Dia. 33

The sequence in this diagram is another joseki which is seen quite frequently. The result leaves Black with a solid and secure position while White is left with a wall exerting influence along the right side. However, since Black was in the corner first and White comes away from this sequence with sente it is natural to expect White's position to be less than perfect. That is to say, because of the presence of Black ▲, there is the aji of a Black cut at 'a'.

Dia. 34

Black 1 is a big yose (end game) move and it is almost mandatory for White to respond by capturing the one Black stone with 2. However, it is aji keshi for Black to play this move too early in the game as now the aji of the cut at 'a' no longer exists. Consequently, yose type moves like Black 1 should be avoided early in the game.

Dia. 35

Another reason why Black need not rush to play 1 in Dia. 34 is that the magari of White 1 in this diagram is gote and Black doesn't have to respond to it unless it is late in the yose stage. The yose situation here is sente-gote for Black. That is, if Black plays 1 in Dia. 34, White must take with 2; on the other hand, if White plays 1 in this diagram, Black will not respond, but will play in another part of the board. Therefore, Black will most likely have the option to play the point 1 at any time he chooses and hence this point can be regarded as being not urgent.

Dia. 36

If Black cuts at 1, White must respond with 2 and Black begins to build a wall along the upper side with the sequence to 5. However, early in the game it is impossible to predict whether this wall will have any effect and it must also be noted that White is making solid territory along the right side while Black is building his wall on the outside. Hence this cut, which tries to utilize the aji of Black ⬤, again must not be played too early in the game.

The next diagram gives an example of the skillful use of the aji resulting from this joseki.

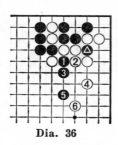

Dia. 36

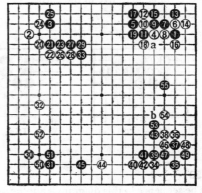

Dia. 37 (1–55)

Dia. 37 Illustrative Game No. 2 (1–55)

This is the first game of the fifth Meijin Sen played August 5 and 6, 1966, between Sakata Eio (Black) and Rin Kai Ho (White). The joseki we have been studying was played in the upper right hand corner from 4 to 19. With the sequence to the magari of 33, Black builds a sizable area on the upper side of the board while White makes territory along the left side. Following this, maneuvers take place on the lower part of the board. Finally, after White 54, Black invades the right side with 55. This move has as its aim both the point 'a', which utilizes the aji of Black 1, and the point 'b', which puts the White group on the right side in jeopardy. That is to say, these points have become miai. Let's consider the meaning of Black 55 in more detail showing how it relates to the aji which exists in the upper right corner.

Dia. 38

In response to Black 1, if White chooses to defend his group on the lower right side by playing 2, Black will cut at 3 utilizing the aji of Black ⬤ in the upper right corner. The sequence up to Black 7 is a natural consequence and Black has succeeded in forming a wall which works very well in conjunction with his two stones marked ⬤ in the center of the board. In addition, Black can aim at the point 'a'

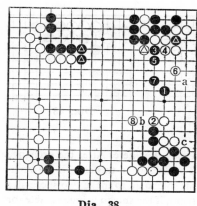

Dia. 38

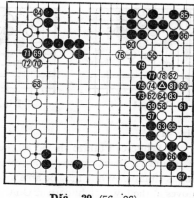

Dia. 39 (56-86)

at some future time thereby reducing any profit White can make on the right side to an absolute minimum. This should be compared with Dia. 36. Next, White can play at 8 or 'b' and Black will either run away or live by starting a ko at 'c'. On the whole, White is not very satisfied with this result.

Dia. 39 (56–86)

As White disliked the prospects of Dia. 38, he played the kaketsugi of 56, thereby correcting the bad aji in the upper right corner. Consequently, Black took the point of 57 and a fierce fight developed on the right side of the board. The sequence continues up to 83 and Black seems to have captured half of the right side while the upper right side becomes White's territory. At this point, Black no longer has a possibility to utilize any other aji in the upper right corner and so after White 84, Black plays 85 and White must capture with 86.

The above is a good example showing how aji can be utilized by employing the concept of miai. Such situations often occur in actual games.

Dia. 40

In this example, we will show a case where White has to make a choice between two different kinds of aji. One involves a ko and the other involves a shicho. In response to White 3, Black will play 4 if he feels that emphasis should be placed on the upper side. After Black 8, White has to choose between 'a' and 'b'.

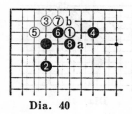

Dia. 40

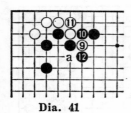

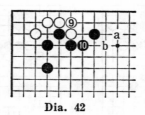

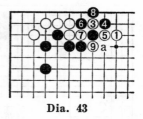

| Dia. 41 | Dia. 42 | Dia. 43 |

Dia. 41

If White can utilize shicho aji, he should play 9 as here. After the exchange of 10 and 11, Black captures one stone with 12 by shicho. In this case, if the situation is suitable, White may be able to utilize this shicho aji to make two successive moves in the lower right corner. On the other hand, if the shicho is unfavorable for Black, he will be forced to play 12 at 'a' and the capture of White 9 is less than perfect.

Dia. 42

Another way is for White simply to respond by connecting with 9. Black will draw back with 10 and the joseki comes to a close. In the future there remains the possibility that a White stone will appear on the points 'a' or 'b'. If this should happen, White will be able to connect it to his stones in the corner.

Dia. 43

To illustrate this connection, suppose White 1 forces Black to respond somewhere else on the board with 2. In that case, the sequence from White 3 to White 9 allows White to connect with ko. However, this ko is almost impossible for Black to win as it is of no use for him to fill this ko at 3. If there is a White stone at 'a' instead of 1, a similar sequence will result.

Dia. 44

After Black 8 in Dia. 40, it is very bad for White to play tsuki-atari with 9. This move is aji keshi since after the sequence to Black 16, there is no bad aji as in Dias. 41 and 42.

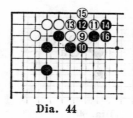

Dia. 44

CHAPTER 3: Kikashi

A kikashi is a forcing move played to produce an effect. That is, a kikashi is a play which must be answered, usually in just one way; the exchange of the kikashi and the answer being useful in some way to the player of the kikashi. The terms kikashi and sente may seem to have the same meaning, but kikashi is applied to moves which are more or less incidental to the main flow of play. Once played, kikashi stones can typically be abandoned without any great loss.

Timing is important in playing kikashi. Usually there is only one correct time play a kikashi for maximum effect, and if this chance is missed it may be lost forever. As the paradigm suggests, "Strike while the iron is hot!"

The following examples will clarify the concept of kikashi as well as demonstrate the effectiveness of such moves.

Dia. 1

The sequence to Black 12 is the beginning of a common joseki. The de of White 9 is an example of a kikashi move and Black must block with 10. If this move were neglected White would push through at the point 10 and Black's loss would be enormous. After Black 12, 'a' becomes the crucial point and White must occupy this point without fail. However, before playing at 'a', White should make some preliminary moves which will give him some profit. Furthermore, the only time he will be able to make such moves is now. If White procrastinates, his chance will be lost forever.

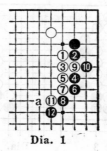

Dia. 1

Dia. 2

First, White cuts with 13 forcing Black to respond by connecting at 14. Next, White utilizes the aji of his stone at 13 and plays another kikashi by attaching at 15. Black has no choice but to reply submissively with 16. Lastly, White again plays kikashi with the ate of 17 and the connection of Black 18 is the only possible reply. Now White finally extends with 19 and because of the aji left behind by White's stone at 17 Black cannot play the forceful oshi at 'b' but must instead submissively draw back with 20. Later in the game White may be able to take the territory in the corner by playing at 'a' but even if this doesn't materialize the presence of White's stone at 15 will effectively keep Black from making any significant profit in the corner. In addition, White 17 still leaves some bad aji behind.

Let's now consider what the outcome would be if White neglected to play kikashi with 13, 15 and 17.

Dia. 3

In response to Black 12, White does not play kikashi as in Dia. 2, but instead immediately extends to 13. In this case Black plays kosumi-tsuke with 14 and White must respond by descending to 15 after which Black connects with 16. With regard to the corner, it is now Black who has the chance to secure territory there by playing at 'b'. Also, there is no bad aji along the right side as there was in Dia. 2 because Black has been able to make a solid connection with 16. Please note that after Black 14, the cut at 'a' no longer has any meaning.

Dia. 4

In response to the cut of White 13, Black must not capture with 14 or he will be completely confined to the side of the board with almost no profit by the sequence to White 21. So, the connection of Black 14 in Dia. 2 is absolutely necessary.

Dia. 5

After connecting at 14, Black need not fear White 15 because he can win the resulting semeai (race to capture) by one move as shown in the sequence to Black 30.

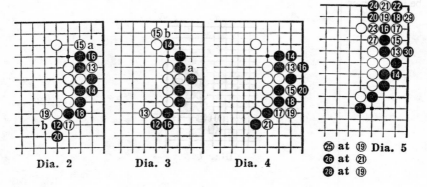

㉕ at ⑲ **Dia. 5**
㉖ at ㉑
㉘ at ⑲

Dia. 2   Dia. 3   Dia. 4

— 20 —

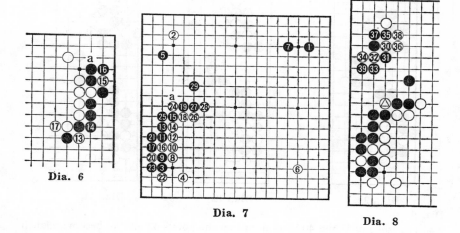

Dia. 6

Dia. 7

Dia. 8

Dia. 6

When playing the kikashi of Dia. 2, White must not reverse the order of moves. If White plays 13 in this diagram first, Black can respond to the cut of 15 by capturing with 16 without any fear of the confinement sequence in Dia. 4. Now a White play at 'a' is no longer kikashi. When playing kikashi, the order of moves must always be carefully considered. In this diagram, White 13 may be kikashi, but it is also aji keshi.

Dia. 7

In this game between two amateur players a joseki similar to the one we have been studying occurred in the lower left corner. However, in response to White 26, Black pushed with 27 followed by the jump of 29. These two moves were not very good as the White stone at 24 creates bad aji for Black along the left side. Of course, in response to White 26, Black should have played 20 in Dia. 2, but even after the hane of White 28, 29 at 'a' would have eliminated the bad aji. In this game, White followed 29 by some very skillful plays and successfully utilized this aji.

Dia. 8

Continuing from Dia. 7, White began by attaching and cutting with 30 and 32, and the sequence to Black 39 seems entirely natural. At this point however, White has a tesuji enabling him to utilize the aji of his stone at ⊘ in conjunction with his two stones at 32 and 34.

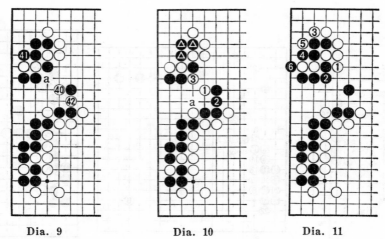

Dia. 9   Dia. 10   Dia. 11

Dia. 9

The tsuke of White 40 is tesuji in that the points 42 and 'a' become miai. If Black plays at 41 to capture two stones, White also takes two stones with 42 and the result is very bad for Black.

Dia. 10

If Black connects at 2 in response to White 1 (White 40 in Dia. 9), White will capture one stone with 3 and Black doesn't have a good response because he must consider both the loss of his three stones marked ⊘ in the corner as well as a White hiki at 'a' which will leave four Black stones drifting in the center. This example again illustrates how the concept of miai comes into play in the utilization of aji.

Dia. 11

The sequence from White 1 to White 5 is tesuji and these moves are also kikashi. However, a line of play like this should be regarded as only a local suji lacking real Go feeling because it does not take into consideration the whole board.

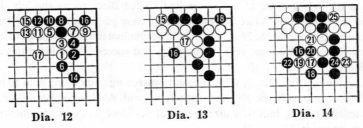

Dia. 12   Dia. 13   Dia. 14

During a game of Go, there often occur moves which seem to be kikashi but are really not. However, if one answers such a move as if it really were kikashi then, in fact, that move becomes kikashi. We will give an example.

Dia. 12

The sequence from White 1 to White 17 is one variation of the small nadare joseki. Because of 17, White's shape in the center is very good. However, Black may try to prevent this with a move that appears to be kikashi.

Dia. 13

Instead of playing 16 as in Dia. 12, Black may try to play 16 as in this diagram. If White, without thinking, submissively plays 17, then 16 will have become kikashi and Black will return to repair the corner with 18. The effect of Black 16 is obvious; it leaves White with a shapeless string of stones on the outside while Black maintains his large profit in the corner when he plays the tsuke of 18.

Dia. 14

In responding to Black 16, White should not let himself be bullied into answering submissively as in Dia. 13 but should counter aggressively with the hane of 17. It is foolish for Black to continue in this manner because after 24, White plays a real kikashi with 23 and then takes the corner with the osae of 25. It should be noted that White 23 has some value in yose and also that the two White stones 17 and 19 can only be captured by shicho. Therefore, should these two stones ever escape, the presence of White 23 causes the Black group on the right side to be eyeless. This may seem, to the average reader, a bit far in the future to consider as a real possibility but this kind of aji must always be borne in mind.

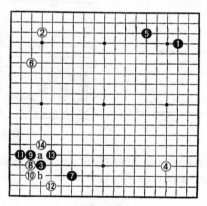

Dia. 15

Dia. 15

This sequence occurred in another game between two amateurs. After the kaketsugi of Black 13, White played nozoki with 14. The question arises as to whether or not this move is kikashi. If Black connects at 'a', it would appear that 14 has accomplished some purpose and has become kikashi. On the other hand, Black may launch a counter-attack by playing 'b', etc. What is Black's correct line of play? Please think about this problem from the point of view of both sente and aji.

Dia. 16

In this case the correct answer is for Black simply to connect with 1. After this, White must make life in the corner with the sequence from 2 to 6. Now Black retains sente and plays a kakari with 7.

Dia. 17

In response to Black 5, White 6 in Dia. 16 cannot be omitted. If White should play 6 as in this diagram, Black will kill the White stones with the sequence from 7 to 11.

Dia. 18

Well, what about the de-giri of Black 1 and 3? After White 4, Black can play shibori with 5 and 7 and as a result, White ⊘ seems to have lost its meaning as kikashi.

Dia. 19

On the other hand, White can live with ease along the lower side, and after the nobi of Black 13, it is White who has sente, allowing him to play 14.

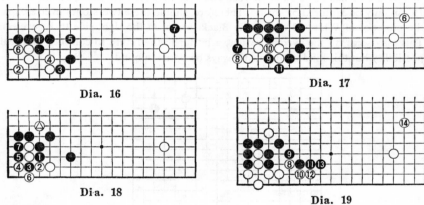

Dia. 16

Dia. 17

Dia. 18

Dia. 19

Dia. 20

The question may arise whether after Black's connection at 1, White couldn't live with the sequence to 6 and then play ogeima at 8.

Dia. 21

If White follows the sequence in Dia. 20 his stones may be alive but not unconditionally. White's aji in the corner is very bad and Black can make ko with the sequence to 5.

— 24 —

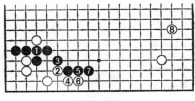

Dia. 20   Dia. 21

Dia. 22

Let us look at this ko under the assumption that White did not play nozoki with 14 in Dia. 15. In this case, after Black 5, White will start the ko with 6 and now the threat of an additional capture at 'a' will make it very difficult for Black to win this ko. That is to say, the pressure will be very great for Black to connect at 'a'. From this point of view, White 14 can be regarded not as kikashi, but as aji keshi, so Black need not regret the fact that he connects at 1 in Dia. 16. Furthermore, the sequence in Dia. 18 is also aji keshi in that Black loses the possible aji of the ko in Dia. 21. So in conclusion, Black 1 in Dia. 16 is the correct answer because White must live in the corner and Black can take sente with 7. On the other hand, if White plays as in Dia. 20 so as to deprive Black of sente, the bad aji left behind will be almost unbearable for White.

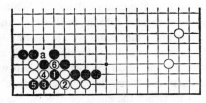

Dia. 22

There is a very thin line between kikashi and aji keshi. Perhaps the main purpose of kikashi is to create aji and in this sense it is different than sente. Hence, moves which have as their consequence the elimination of the opponent's bad aji cannot really be considered kikashi unless they have other, more important, merits. Beginners usually cannot fathom this interrelationship and just as one often sees a weak player submissively following a stronger player around the board dutifully answering every move in the most obvious way, one also sees players who at every opportunity play atari, nozoki, etc., under the mistaken impression that these are kikashi moves, when, in fact, they only strengthen the opponents' stones and achieve no compensating advantage whatsoever.

The following examples illustrate the thinking which goes into deciding whether or not to play kikashi.

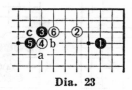

Dia. 23

Dia. 23

Consider this niken basami joseki. After White plays 6, Black has to decide between three main plays: ate at 'a', ate at 'b', or tsugi at 'c'. But what is the reasoning behind this? Why shouldn't Black play at 'a' or 'b' before connecting at 'c'? Isn't this kikashi? Certainly, one thing is immediately clear; Black must eventually defend the cutting point of 'c' after the osae of White 6. That is, if Black plays ate at 'a', White connects at 'b' and Black connects at 'c'. On the other hand, if Black 'b', White 'a' and again Black 'c'. However, at this stage of the game it is impossible to tell which of these two ways is best. Furthermore, suppose Black first connects at 'c'. There are now two possible moves for White; nobi at 'a' or tsugi at 'b'. If White plays at 'a', the kikashi will disappear, but Black has sente and there is still the cutting point at 'b' left behind as aji. On the other hand, if White connects at 'b', Black can take sente and play some other point or he can play at 'a' which reverts back to the case of Black 'a', White 'b', Black 'c'. Consequently, Black has no need to play kikashi in this case and so connects at 'c' in response to White 6. The important point we are making is that when deciding whether to play kikashi or not, one must decide if it will add to his advantage sufficiently to compensate for the resultant loss of options which were available. Hence, as this example illustrates, Black, by connecting at 'c' and refraining from playing ate at 'a' or 'b', can retain the effect of at least one of these two kikashi. This example will be further developed in the problem section.

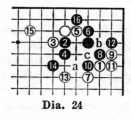

Dia. 24

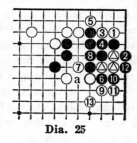

Dia. 25

Dia. 24

This situation is a rather common double kakari joseki against a Black stone at hoshi. In this sequence, Black must end in gote by playing the hane of 16. This is because there is still some bad aji in the corner; that is, a White play at 'b' will place Black's stone at 8 in atari. Also, please note that a White play at 'a' seems to be kikashi in that Black must respond by playing at 'c'. However, this move if played prior to Black 16 is aji keshi in that it will make Black 16 unnecessary.

Dia. 25

Suppose Black neglects to play 16 in Dia. 24. In that case, White will play hasami-tsuke with 1. After Black 2, the nozoki of White 3 forces Black to connect at 4 allowing White to connect underneath with 5. Next, Black plays 6 in order to capture the three White stones marked ◭. This is the perfect time for White to play 7 which is now really kikashi. This is White's last chance to play this move because when the three White stones ◭ are gone, it can not be played with sente. In addition, this move is necessary since a Black play at 'a' becomes a threat after Black 6. White 7 corrects this defect. Finally, White plays shibori with 9 and 11 forcing Black to capture with 10 and 12, after which White makes good shape with 13. White has also invaded Black's corner while Black still needs one more move to make two eyes to ensure the life of his group. Consequently, it is concluded that Black 16 in Dia. 24 must not be omitted.

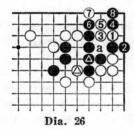

Dia. 26

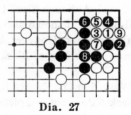

Dia. 27

Dia. 26

What would the situation be if, in the course of the joseki of Dia. 25, White exchanged ◯ for ●. This would not be kikashi, but aji keshi. In this case, Black can descend to 2 in response to the attachment of White 1 and now White 3 does not threaten atari at 'a'. Therefore, Black has a free move and he can play the tesuji at 4. White's resistance to 7 is futile since Black captures the corner with 8.

Dia. 27

This diagram shows that White's method in Dia. 26 does not work if ◯ and ● in that diagram haven't been exchanged.

Up to this point we have given examples of kikashi involving close in-fighting of stones. However, the concept of kikashi is more general and often occurs in strategic planning as the following example shows.

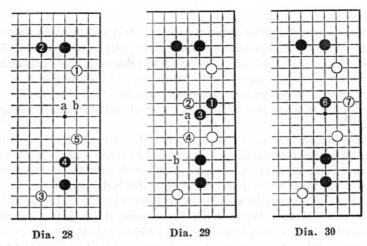

Dia. 28   Dia. 29   Dia. 30

Dia. 28

The sequence to White 5 is often seen in four-stone handicap games. Black's best procedure is to invade on the right side now. But which is better, 'a' or 'b'?

Dia. 29

If Black plunges in too deeply with 1, White will play boshi with 2 and after the kosumi of Black 3, White jumps to 4 threatening to play 'a' or 'b' which have now become miai. Although Black 1 may not be necessarily bad, it can lead to very complicated fighting. It should also be mentioned that other moves in addition to 3 are available to Black. However, by showing this sequence we are only trying to give a sense of the feeling of Black 1.

Dia. 30

After White 5 in Dia. 28, the invasion of Black 6 on the fourth line is recommended. Black 6 does not completely separate the two White stones on the right side since White can connect underneath by sliding to 7. However, this move is a bit submissive and makes Black 6 a kind of kikashi.

Dia. 31

Consider the following hypothetical sequence after White 7. Black extends to 8 whereupon White jumps to 9. Black 10 is a natural response and after 11 Black plays kosumi-tsuke with 12 (also kikashi) forcing White to play sagari with 13. Now Black could run away at 15, but let us suppose he abandons his kikashi stone and plays ikken tobi at 14, which is natural. If White plays 15, then Black ● seems to have lost most of its usefulness, but then so has White 7, so Black does not mind. Furthermore, there remains the aji of Black 'a', White 'b' and Black 'c'.

Dia. 32

Instead of playing 7 in Dia. 30, White immediately plays the sequence from 1 to 7. This is the same as Dia. 31 with the exception that Black doesn't have a stone at 'a' and White doesn't have a stone at 'b'. From this hypothetical analysis it is easy to see why Black 6 in Dia. 30 effectively separates the two White stones.

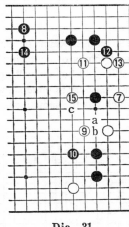

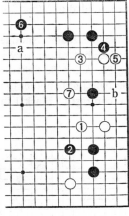

Dia. 31   Dia. 32

Dia. 33 Illustrative Game No. 3 (1–38)

This is the fourth game of the 1968 Honinbo Sen. Black was Rin Kai Ho and White was Sakata Eio, who was Honinbo at that time. With 37, Black threatens to make a huge territory along the lower side. White plays 38 so as to reduce this area. Now, how should Black respond?

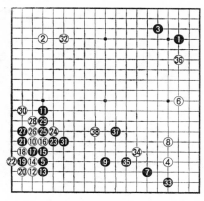

Dia. 33 (1—38)

— 29 —

Dia. 34

Black 1 is a very big move which secures the territory along the lower side. However, when Black plays in this way, White ⊘ becomes kikashi. Since there is no longer any chance to invade the lower side after Black 1, White plays the hane-tsugi of 2 and 4, against which Black must connect at 5 to avoid any further incursion into his area. For Black to play 1 is not bad but it lacks spirit. Let's see how Rin Kai Ho responded to White 38 of Dia. 33.

Dia. 35 (38–40)

In the actual game, Black responded to White 38 with the keima of 39. This move is not submissive, but rather very aggressive and thinks of capturing the whole side including 38. A terrific fight ensued with White 40 but we will postpone an analysis of this fight until another time. However, please try to understand the spirit of Black 39 in contrast to Black 1 in Dia. 34 which has the same feeling as White 7 in Dia. 30.

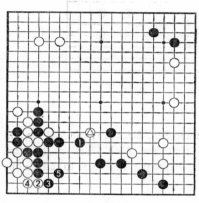

Dia. 34

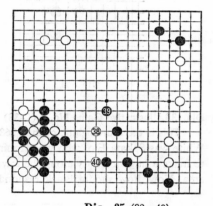

Dia. 35 (38—40)

CHAPTER 4: Thickness

The word thickness, as used in Go, is approximately synonymous with strength. A group of stones is thick if it contains few or no weak points and is not vulnerable to attack. It should be obvious that thickness is a good thing to have. Your opponent must be extremely cautious in the vicinity of your thickness, for he will not find any useful kikashi to play against it should his stones get into trouble. Backed up by thickness, you can attack with carefree abandon. Also, in a ko fight the player whose groups are thick will have the advantage. Hence, in the first half of the game, building thickness is just as important as making territory.

The key idea in handling thickness is to treat it with respect and not to play too close to it, whether it be your opponent's thickness or your own. Let us look at some examples which illustrates this principle.

Dia. 1

This example is taken from a game between Sakata (White) and Hoshino, 8-dan. The White group in the lower right is extremely thick. How should White play? White 1 in this diagram is much too close to the White thickness. Clearly Black 2 is a larger move than White 1.

Dia. 2

Sakata chose to invade at 1, and the sequence up to 19 is what was played in the actual game. Black had some difficulty finding severe moves. Due to the presence of White's thickness he had to make defensive plays at 2 and 18, and the invasion was a success for White. Note that 'a' still remains as a large yose point for him.

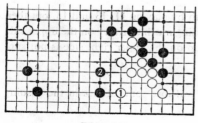

Dia. 1

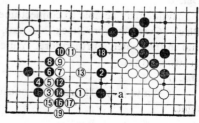

Dia. 2

Dia. 3

If Black had used 18 in the last diagram to capture three stones, as with 1 in this diagram, he would have suffered a big loss. White 2 captures a large territory. It is pointless for Black to extend into the teeth of White's thickness with 3. White 4, in conjunction with White's thickness, deprives Black of eyes. The reader should work out the details for himself.

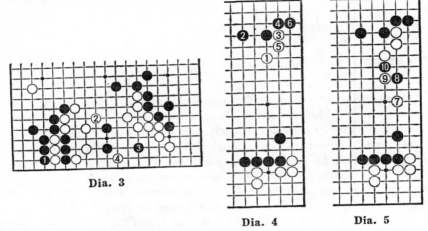

Dia. 3

Dia. 4

Dia. 5

When your opponent has made thickness, you should try to deal with it by establishing some stones a safe distance away from it. After making such a base, you can approach more closely.

Dia. 4

In this diagram, taken from a game between a professional player and a strong amateur, Black has played a joseki in the lower right which gives him thickness in exchange for corner territory. White plays 1, 3 and 5 in line with the strategy just described. Now where should White play 7?

Dia. 5

In the absence of the stones in the lower right, White 7 is joseki, but in the present circumstances Black can invade at 8, threatening to capture White 7. After White 9 and Black 10, White is in trouble.

Dia. 6

White may be able to connect underneath by playing 11, 13 and 15, but then Black 16 creates more Black thickness, promising much territory on the upper side and in the center. Furthermore, White's group on the upper right side is not sure of two eyes yet.

Dia. 7

If White plays 11 from the outside, he will lose some stones in the ensuing fight.

Dia. 8

Considering this, the professional player (Ishida Yoshio, the present Honinbo) extended only as far as 7 in this diagram. This gave him safety, and later he had a chance to approach closer to Black's thickness by playing 'a'.

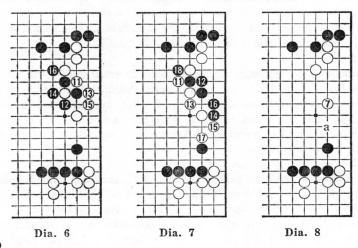

Dia. 6   Dia. 7   Dia. 8

Dia. 9

In response to White 1, the niken takabasami of Black 2 in conjunction with Black ⬤ is a good strategy. The 3–3 invasion of the corner with White 3 is the usual continuation and with the sequence to 8, Black has made thickness on the outside while White has taken profit in the corner. Black ⬤ has now become an ideally placed stone as it is a good extension from both the shimari in the upper right corner and the wall on the lower right side.

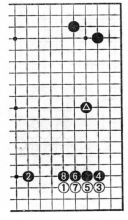

Dia. 9

Dia. 10

However, if Black has no stone at 'a' or the point 9, Black 2 is not a good move. Now after the sequence to Black 8, White makes a wedge between the two Black positions with 9, nullifying the effect of Black's wall on the lower right side. When Black plays 2, he is aiming to make thickness, placing no emphasis on the area in the corner, so before making this move he must make certain that, strategically, this thickness will have some value.

Dia. 11

Because of circumstances which often occur in actual games, it is not always possible to obtain an ideal placement of stones as in Dia. 9. Consider, for example, the situation in this diagram. Black has made a very impressive thickness on the lower right side of the board. However, White has been able apparently to nullify this thickness by making a wedge at 1. What method should Black adopt to make the best use of this thickness?

Dia. 12

It is nonsense for Black to play the tsume of 2 in answer to White 1. This move provokes the extension of White 3 which not only lets White make good shape on the right side but also weakens Black's "secure" corner. In addition, Black 2 is too close to his thick wall of stones and does not utilize them in an efficient manner. That is, for the number of stones invested, Black 2 does not form enough territory. Black 2 violates one of the principles of thickness, i.e. "Don't use thickness to form territory."

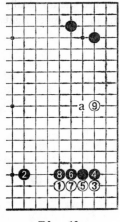

Dia. 10

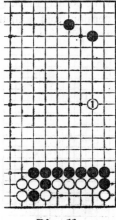

Dia. 11

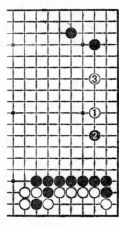

Dia. 12

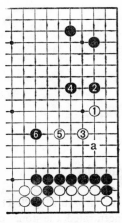

Dia. 13

Dia. 13

One of the strategic principles of Go is "Drive your opponent in the direction of your strong stones and not in the direction of your weak ones." Since the Black thickness on the lower right side is stronger than the shimari in the upper right corner, it is clear that the tsume of Black 2 follows this principle. White 3 illustrates the counter-principle in regard to thickness; that is, "Don't approach thickness too directly." In other words, "Don't bash your head against a stone wall." Also, 3 allows White to run away easily into the center with 5. However, a simple extension to 'a' would not have left this good move available. Next, the boshi of 6 seems to be the most logical way for Black to continue the attack.

As a result of the tsume of 2 and the tobi of 4, Black has been able to make an ideal shape in conjunction with his shimari in the upper right corner. Furthermore, the White stones are still weak because of the powerful influence of the Black thickness which may permit him to gain more profit by continuing the attack with 6.

In Part II of this book many problems concerning thickness will be presented and the reader will be able to gain practice in using the above-mentioned principles.

CHAPTER 5: Korigatachi

Literally, korigatachi means "frozen shape". This term refers to a configuration of stones which is overconcentrated, the stones of this configuration not being used to their maximum efficiency. Dia. 1 shows a simple example of korigatachi.

Dia. 1 Inefficient

White has formed a two point extension on the third line. In this situation, it is almost a formula for Black to play kikashi with the kosumi-tsuke of 1 forcing White to play 2. Now White ⬡ is too close to his two stone wall and his shape becomes korigatachi. This stone would be more efficiently placed at 'a' or 'b'.

Dia. 2 Ideal shape

If Black neglects to play the exchange of 1 for 2 in Dia. 1, White will exchange 1 for 2 as in this diagram and now his shape on the lower side is ideal.

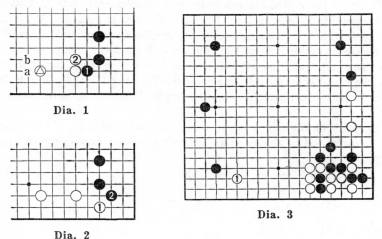

Dia. 1

Dia. 2

Dia. 3

Dia. 3

White has just played kakari with 1. How should Black respond so as to force White into korigatachi?

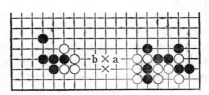

Dia. 5

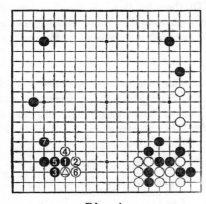

Dia. 4

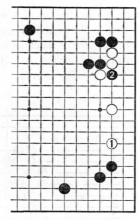

Dia. 6

Dia. 4

In response to White ⬨, Black should play tsuke-osae with 1 and 3. The sequence to Black 7, which is joseki, will follow, leaving Black with a large profit in the corner and White with thickness along the lower side. But what is this thickness worth?

Dia. 5

If White were to make an extension from his formation on the lower left side, the ideal point would be at 'a'. On the other hand, the ideal point for an extension from the formation on the lower right side would be at 'b'. The sphere of influence of these two formations overlap on the points marked ×. Eventually, White may have to play on one of these points to prevent Black from invading. But, for White to play on one of the points × will result in korigatachi.

Dia. 6

White has just played tsume with 1 against which Black replies by cutting at 2. What is the meaning of this cut?

Dia. 7

When Black cuts with 2, he is expecting White to play ate with 3. After the exchange of 4 for 5, Black plays kikashi with 6, 8 and 10 forcing White to take the two stones 2 and 4. These kikashi moves are very useful in that Black is able to make a solid wall without any bad aji. On the other hand, White ⊘ is now too close to the White wall of 7, 5 and 3. This stone would be more efficiently placed at 'a'. White ⊘, placed as in this diagram, puts too many stones in one area and causes an over-concentration of stones.

Dia. 8

In response to the cut of Black 2, in order to avoid the korigatachi which results in Dia. 7, White should play 3 and 5. Now White ⊘ is efficiently placed, blocking the advance of Black's stones at 2 and 4. Furthermore, Black still has bad aji in his wall at 'a' leaving the point 'b' for White to aim at.

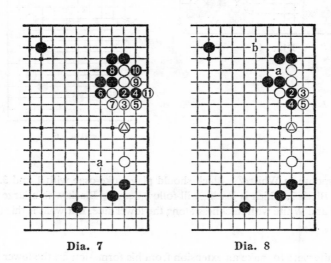

Dia. 7   Dia. 8

In the example of Dia. 7, the aji of the Black stones at 2 and 4 in conjunction with the kikashi moves of 6, 8 10 were important for causing the resulting korigatachi. In fact, kikashi is often the key for causing one's opponent to make korigatachi. In Dia. 8, by not allowing Black to play kikashi, White was able efficiently to utilize all his stones and still preserve Black's bad aji. Another example will now be given to emphasize the relationship between these two concepts.

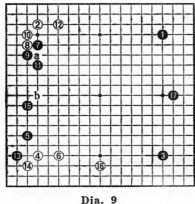

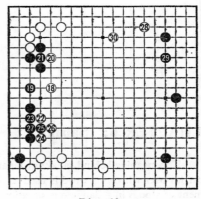

Dia. 9   Dia. 10

Dia. 9

In this fuseki, Black's moves from 11 to 15 are a bit dubious. It would have been better for Black to have played 11 at 'a' immediately followed by 'b'. This would have resulted in a well-balanced shape on the left side for Black. However, after Black 17, White can force Black into korigatachi on the left side by some well-timed kikashi moves.

Dia. 10

White plays kikashi with 18, 20, 22, etc. followed by 28 and 30. This results in Black's being pressed into a low position on the left side. This low position leaves the feeling that Black is not getting enough territory for the stones invested; that is to say, these stones are overconcentrated. White, on the other hand, is beginning to form a wall along the entire left side and this potential wall will have a strategic influence throughout the middle stage of this game. It might be noted that White 24 is not really kikashi and this move should be played at a later time. It was given here only to emphasize the feeling of the left side. The point 24, however, can be considered White's option as it is hard to imagine Black making a meaningful move in this area of the board.

CHAPTER 6: Sabaki

The meaning behind sabaki in Japanese is "development". This same meaning carries over when this word is used as a Go term. In Go, it refers to the development of stones in a dangerous situation in a kind of quick, light and flexible way, either to escape or to make eyes if necessary. Consider the following example.

Dia. 1

Black has just played at ⚫ threatening to capture four White stones by playing at 'a'. In addition, the two White stones in the corner do not yet have a living shape.

Dia. 2

The geta of White 1 seems to be the most obvious way for White to proceed. If Black attacks the corner with the hane-tsugi of 2 and 4, White intends to live by playing 3 and 5. However, 5 forces Black to play nobi with 6 and now the same four White stones, △, are in trouble again since Black can capture them by playing at 'a'. On the other hand, if White defends against this threat by playing 'a', Black will play osae at 'b' and the White stones in the corner die. However, White has a way to save the four stones marked △ as well as the two stones in the corner.

Dia. 3

The correct procedure for White to follow is to dispose of the corner with the kikashi of 1, 3 and 5. In this way, White is able to give his stones in the corner a living shape without causing damage to the outside stones. In addition, White retains sente with which he can defend his endangered stones by playing geta with 7.

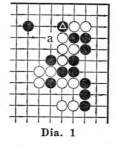

Dia. 1

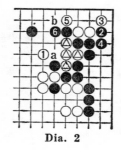

Dia. 2

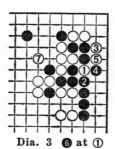

Dia. 3 ⑥ at ①

The White moves from 1 to 7 are an example of sabaki. Please note that sabaki does not refer to shape; rather, it is a way of playing. However, the idea of shape is often related to the method of sabaki. Sabaki is often used to avoid omoi katachi (heavy shape). A group of stones having a heavy shape is unwieldy and susceptible to attack. The method of sabaki can be used in such cases to prevent stones from becoming heavy, allowing the formation of eyes to be easily attained.

Dia. 4

Consider the situation in the upper right corner. It is Black's turn to play. How should he prevent White from making sabaki?

Dia. 5

The kosumi-tsuke of Black 1 forces White to play tachi with 2. From this formation, White, in order to make an ideal shape, would like to play at either 'a' or 'b'. However, it is Black's turn to play and he attacks with a severe hasami at 3. With this move, the two White stones take on a heavy shape and cannot easily make eyes.

Dia. 6

However, if Black reverses the order of moves and plays at 1 first, White can expand his corner by playing sabaki with 2, 4, 6 and 8. Playing in this way, White can get at least one eye after which he can run away lightly into the center with 10.

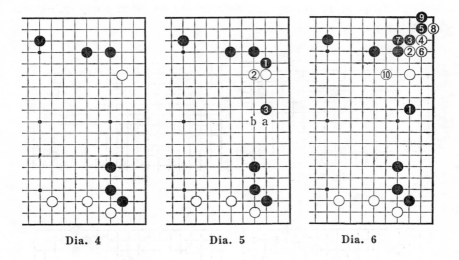

Dia. 4   Dia. 5   Dia. 6

The method of sabaki, although it often occurs in joseki, is essentially a middle game technique. Its most frequent application is to be found in the invasion and reduction of large territorial frameworks. When disposing of such structures, the method of sabaki is a very useful technique.

Dia. 7

In the upper right quarter of the board, Black has formed a double-wing formation based on a kogeima shimari. In such a case, the vital point of both defense and attack is at White 1. In response to 1, Black usually plays at either 'a' or 'b'. For the sake of discussion, suppose Black answers at 'a'.

Dia. 8

After the keima of Black 2, the attachment of White 3 and the cut of White 5 are standard procedure. After Black plays 6, White will play kikashi with 7 and 9 forcing Black to capture one stone with 10. Finally, White runs away lightly with 11, having established a foothold, albeit a thin one, on the upper side. In addition, the Black stone, ⬤, has been isolated.

Dia. 9

Some readers may wonder about White 11 in Dia. 8. Since there are many cutting points in the White formation one might think it better for White to defend more directly with a move like the kaketsugi of 1 in this diagram. However, if White plays in this way, Black will play nozoki with 2, a kikashi move which forces White to connect at 3. This kikashi prevents White from making an eye at 2, thereby leaving him with a heavy shape.

Dia. 10

To connect with a katatsugi at 1 is even worse for White. Black strikes at White's vital point for making eyes, again leaving the White group eyeless and heavy.

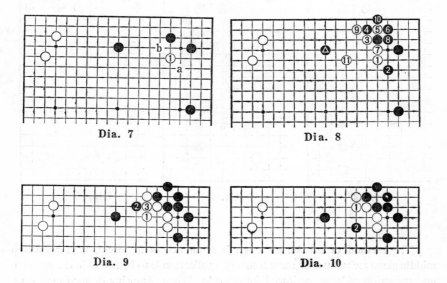

Dia. 7   Dia. 8

Dia. 9   Dia. 10

Dia. 11

White 11 in Dia. 8 is the essence of what is called karui sabaki (light sabaki). White 3, 5, 7 and 9 are all, in a sense, kikashi and White intends to utilize these stones in conjunction with 11 to make good shape on the outside. For this reason, White does not fear the cut of Black 1 in this diagram. In fact, he welcomes it. In response, White plays ate at 2 and after Black captures one stone with 3, White plays magari with 4. If Black continues in this way by capturing another stone with 5, White will play nobi with 6. The point to understand here is that while Black is focusing his attention on capturing stones (note that each move is worth only from one to two points), White is becoming thicker and thicker on the outside and Black ⬤ is becoming weaker and weaker, gradually falling under the shadow of the growing White thickness. It should also be noted that White at 'a' will probably be answered by Black's capturing one stone at 'c'. However, White must not rush to play this point since 'b' also forces Black to capture at 'c'. This aji must be left till later because White doesn't know which move will become more important as the game develops. However, if Black foolishly plays at 'b', White will extend to 'd' and now a White move at 'a' is no longer aji keshi. This example illustrates an important point about kikashi: One should not place any importance on stones which have been used as kikashi. Instead, they should be utilized for the aji they have created and sacrificed without regret. Please notice that White Ⓐ also effectively prevents Black from breaking out into the center.

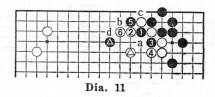

Dia. 11

Diagrams 7, 8, 9, 10 and 11 shows how sabaki is used to reduce potentially large territorial structures which often occur in the middle game. However, the method of sabaki also occurs in the fuseki stage and is used when a player must develop his stones quickly.

Dia. 12

This example was taken from a game between two amateur players. After the kakari of White 18, Black attaches with 19. Considering the presence of a Black stone at 17 and the Black thickness on the lower left, how should White play next?

Dia. 13

The hane of White 1 and the kaketsugi of White 3 are the most common ways for White to respond to the tsuke of Black 19 in Dia. 12. However because of the presence of Black ⓐ on the right side, Black can immediately begin an attack with 4. The sequence to White 13 is a well-known joseki, but in this case it turns out very badly for White. Black has made territory on the right side as well as the beginnings of a large prospective territory on the lower side, while White's stones have only just managed to escape. So we must conclude that White 3 was a mistake. What should he have played?

Dia. 14

After White plays kikashi with 1 the correct continuation is to jump lightly to 3. This way is sabaki. What happens now?

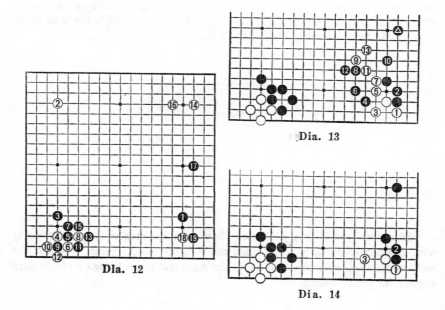

Dia. 13

Dla. 12

Dia. 14

— 44 —

Dia. 15

Black 4 and 6 are very sluggish moves. In response, White again jumps lightly to 5 and plays kikashi at 7 forcing Black to capture at 8. After this, White has sente and can make another move elsewhere on the board. So, while Black is nibbling away at the lower right corner, White is developing very quickly.

Dia. 16

The result in Dia. 15 is very bad for Black, so in response to White 3 in Dia. 13, he should play tsume with 4 against which White descends to 5. When compared with Dia. 13, it is clearly seen that this result is good for White. White's stones are alive in the corner with good future endgame possibilities along the lower right side. In addition, the Black area on the lower side is still very thin. Considering Black's initial advantage in this portion of the board, White can consider his intrusion a success.

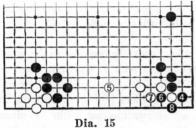

Dia. 15

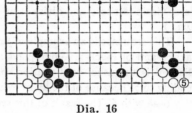

Dia. 16

From the above examples it is seen that sabaki consists of two steps: first, kikashi moves and then the moves which occupy vital points. The kikashi moves usually turn out to be blocking moves in that the opponent must, in a sense, go around them in order to attack the main body of stones. In the meantime, the player of sabaki will be developing his stones at a very quick pace. It can be easily understood from this why sabaki is so useful in attacking formations that have already been built up to an extent.

CHAPTER 7: Furikawari

Furikawari means "exchange." It can happen anytime in the course of a game when one player takes territory (real or potential) that belongs to the other player and, in exchange, gives up some of his own. Sometimes, both players simply enter virgin territory and divide it up as in the following example.

Dia. 1

This sequence is an example of furikawari in a joseki. In response to the niken takabasami of Black 2, White plays a counter hasami with 3. The attachment of Black 4 is the usual continuation, but now White initiates a furikawari by extending to 5. Because of the aji of White's stone at 1, Black has little choice but to play osae with 6. The result of this sequence is furikawari in that White has given up the territory in the corner in order to establish a position along the right side. Although Black's profit in the corner is fairly large, such a procedure may be justified if the right side is important to White.

Dia. 2

This is another niken takabasami joseki. After the kake of White 3, Black plays degiri with 4 and 6. At this point, White shifts the scene of the struggle to the upper side by playing tsuke with 7. However, Black focuses his attention on the right side and plays nobi with 8. When White plays nobi with 9, Black plays 10, eliminating the bad aji of the White stone at 3, and with 11 the joseki comes to a close with Black taking the right side while White establishes himself on the upper side.

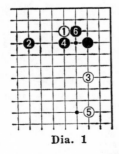

Dia. 1

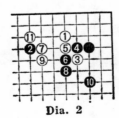

Dia. 2

Dia. 3

In response to the tsuke of White 7, the nobi of Black 8 in Dia. 2 is almost forced. If instead Black plays tachi with 8 as in this diagram, White will play the ate-de tesuji of 9 and 11. The sequence ends with Black 16, but this is gote for Black. However, when Black simply follows the sequence in Dia. 2, he retains sente. Hence, Black 8 in this diagram must be rejected.

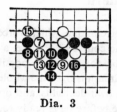

Dia. 3

Furikawari sequences always have a stone (or stones) around which the moves focus. This stone has aji which one must eliminate while the other player threatens, from a distance, to make this aji come to life. White 1 in Dia. 1 and White 3 in Dia. 2 are examples of stones having such aji. In both instances Black must spend two moves eliminating their aji but, in the meantime, White is building up his position elsewhere. This is similar to the situation which was seen in the section on sabaki. In that case there was the aji of the kikashi stones which had to be overcome before the main stones could be attacked. However, while one player was nibbling away at these kikashi stones, the other player was developing elsewhere on the board. To be precise, sabaki is a method of playing while furikawari refers to a result. Actually, in a general sense, the examples of Dias. 1 and 2 in this section are sabaki sequences which result in furikawari.

CHAPTER 8: Yosu-miru

Yosu-miru is a probing technique which forces one's opponent to fix the shape of his stones. During the course of a game, a player naturally tries to keep his options as flexible as possible for as long as possible in order to take advantage of the constantly fluctuating situation over the whole board. When making a yosu-miru move, one maintains his own flexibility and options but forces his opponent to settle on a particular shape before he is ready to, thereby reducing his options. There may be a number of ways to respond to a yosu-miru move, but once the shape is fixed, the other player can plan his strategy on the basis of this fixed shape.

The technique of yosu-miru is perhaps the most difficult one to master as it makes use of all the concepts we have studied in the preceding chapters, especially aji, kikashi and sabaki. It is also requires a great deal of judgment and intuition.

Dia. 1 Illustrative Game No. 4 (1–18)

This game is taken from the sixth game of the 1968 Honinbo Sen between Sakata Eio (White) and Rin Kai Ho (Black). With the kosumi of White 18, the fuseki comes to an end. Black would now like to play ikken tobi at 'a'. However, this move is a bit slow and White would respond by playing kikashi at 'b', Black 'c', followed by White 'd' which forms a very large prospective area for White on the upper side. Consequently, Black must somehow dispose of the upper side.

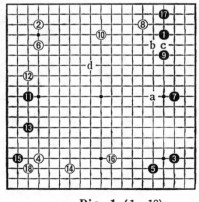

Dia. 1 (1 –18)

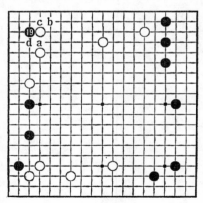

Dia. 2 (19)

Dia. 2

Black begins his invasion by attaching at 19. This move is yosu-miru. Its purpose is to see how White intends to defend this sector of the board. Depending on how White responds, Black will plan his strategy. White has four ways to answer; the connection of 'a', the kosumi of 'b', the descent of 'c', and the osae of 'd'.

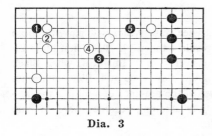

Dia. 3

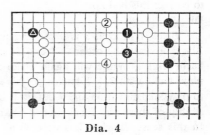

Dia. 4

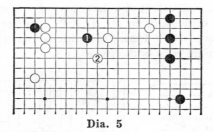

Dia. 5

Dia. 3

In response to Black 1, White connects at 2. This move indicates that White intends to place emphasis on the outside. Hence, Black counters this intention by playing kikashi at 3, forcing White to defend with 4. Next, Black invades with 5 and this is the natural continuation.

Dia. 4

The invasion of Black 5 in Dia. 3 is a very important point. However, the kikashi of Black 3 must precede that move. If, after playing at ◉, Black rushes to play 1 immediately, as in this diagram, White will play 2 and 4 building up an impressive territory along the upper left side. Black 3 in Dia. 3 prevents this White expansion.

Dia. 5

For Black to invade at 1 is an overplay. This invasion is too deep and Black will be severely attacked with the keima of White 2.

Dia. 6

After White plays 2 in Dia. 3, it may seem that Black has abandoned his stone at 1 when he plays 3 and 5 in that diagram. However, this is not the case since the aji in the corner is bad for White. Black can live in the corner by ko with the sequence from 1 to 7. This is a very difficult ko for White since, if Black wins this ko by capturing at 'a', White's area on the upper side will be in danger of complete annihilation. So, the presence of this potential ko will be a thorn in White's side as long as it exists and he will eventually have to lose a move by going back to correct this bad aji.

Dia. 7

Black 1 in Dia. 3 is a probing move to see how White will play. Suppose Black reversed the order of 1 and 3; what would happen? If Black first plays kikashi with 1, White will again obediently answer with 2. But now, when Black plays tsuke with 3, White changes his tactics and plays osae at 4. Black continues to play kikashi with 5 and 7 but now, because of the presence of White 2, the possibility of these two Black stones making life or escaping becomes more difficult. In this sense, Black 1 has become aji keshi.

Dia. 8

If White responds to Black ⬤ with the kosumi of 1, Black will invade with 2. If White defends the corner with the osae of 3, Black will play hane-tsugi with 4 and 6 followed by the oshi of 8. Instead of 8, Black could make watari at 'a', but 8 seems to be more in the spirit of this game.

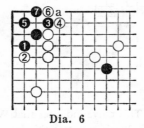

Dia. 6

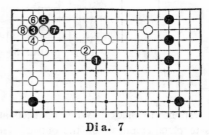

Dia. 7

Dia. 9

In response to Black 2, it is not advisable for White to try to confine Black with the oshi of 3. In this case, Black will live in the corner with the sequence to 12. The size of this corner is at least 10 points and this is too big for White to allow. Although the Black stones on the lower left side have become weaker, Black can ensure their life rather easily. However, please note that this sequence is not possible if White has a stone at 'a'.

Dia. 10

Against the sagari of White 1, Black will again play uchikomi with 2 and the sequence is the same as in Dia. 8.

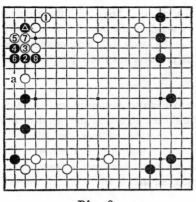

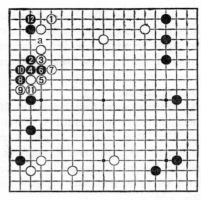

Dia. 8   Dia. 9

Dia. 11 (19–25)

In the actual game, White played the osae of 20 in response to Black 19. By playing this move, White indicates his determination to keep the corner. Hence, Black shifts his attention to the outside but utilizes the aji of Black 19 to make a tentative position with 21 and 23. These two moves are kikashi and together with the extension of 25 comprise a sabaki sequence. At this point, Black's maneuvers on the upper left side come to an end and he should be satisfied with this result.

After White 18 in Dia. 1, Black is faced with the problem of how to invade the upper side. The tsuke of 19 is a probing move which seeks out White's future intentions. If White connects at 2 as in Dia. 3, it means White places emphasis on the outside. On the other hand, the osae of 20 in Dia. 11 shows White's intention to secure the corner. In both these cases, Black adopted appropriate counter-measures. In addition, there are the kosumi of White 1 in Dia. 8 and the sagari of White 1 in Dia. 10. Both these moves give Black an opportunity to invade at 2 (please study the comment about White 'a' in Dia. 9 to understand this) thereby building up a sizeable area on the left side.

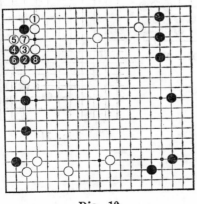

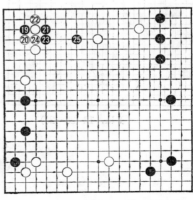

Dia. 10   Dia. 11 (19—25)

To continue, after Black 25 in Dia. 11, White is now faced with the problem of how to attack the Black formation on the right side of the board. Where should he begin? Should he invade the upper right side, the lower right side, or should he attack the shimari in the lower right corner? This problem was also solved by a yosu-miru move.

Dia. 12 (26–28)

White attached from below with 26. This move is also yosu-miru against which Black played the nobi of 27. As a result, White shifted his attack and invaded with 28. Why? Because Black 27 placed emphasis on outside influence, but White ⊘ is situated so as to have a nullifying effect on this influence. Furthermore, the aji in the corner is bad for Black since White can easily live there. Consequently, since the lower right side is pretty much settled, all that is left is the invasion of White 28.

Dia. 13

As mentioned in Dia. 12, White can live in the corner anytime he wishes by playing 1, 3 and 5. If Black continues to attack with 6, 8 and 10, White will defend with the moves up to 11. However, White ends in gote so the time to play this sequence must be carefully considered.

Dia. 14

Besides Black 27 in Dia. 12, there are four other ways for him to respond; at 'a', 'b', 'c' and 'd'. Let's consider each of these moves.

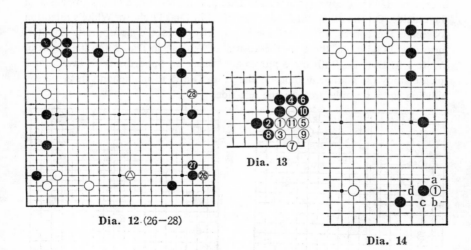

Dia. 12 (26–28)

Dia. 13

Dia. 14

Dia. 15

First of all, there is the osae of Black 2 in response to White 1. In this case, White cuts with 3 and when Black plays ate with 4, White plays sabaki with the kikashi of 5 and 7 followed by a light play at 9. After this, White will aim at an invasion around the point 'a' or attack Black's stones on the upper side with the kosumi of 'b'. In any case, White accomplishes his purpose by establishing a foothold on the right side.

Dia. 16

Needless to say, White has no fear of a Black cut at 1. In reply, White would play one ate with 2 followed by another with 4 making good shape. If Black plays 3 at 4, White will answer at 'a'.

Dia. 17

The second alternative is for Black to play osae from the inside with 2. Again White plays sabaki with the kikashi of 3 followed by the tobi of 5 and 6. This result is quite satisfactory for White.

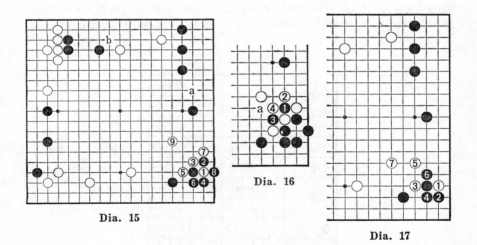

Dia. 15

Dia. 16

Dia. 17

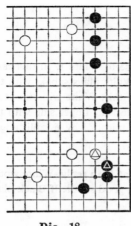

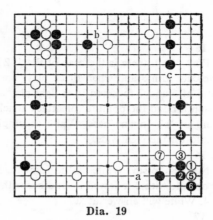

Dia. 19

Dia. 18

Dia. 18

This is a tewari diagram. It is obtained by removing the kikashi stones of Dia. 17 and their replies. In this way the real value of the moves made becomes clear. By this we see that in reply to White ⬡, Black played ▲, which is not really a very good move. This should give the reader a deeper insight into the value of kikashi.

Dia. 19

The next variation is the hiki of Black 2. White responds with the hane of 3. Black 4 is a severe move, but White plays 5 and then jumps to 7. In this case, since Black's corner is vulnerable, White 'a' is sente. In addition, White can also aim at the points 'b' and 'c'.

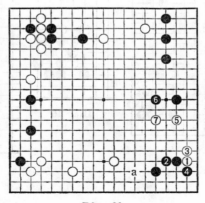

Dia. 20

Dia. 20

Finally, there is the hiki-age of Black 2. When White plays 3, Black can play osae with 4. Next White jumps to 5 and after Black 6, White also jumps to 7. In this case, Black's aji in the corner is bad and the White tsume of 'a' is almost sente.

Dia. 21

In answer to White 3, Black could also play kake with 4, confining White to the side and corner. However, White makes a large life in the corner with the sequence to 9 and White is not dissatisfied.

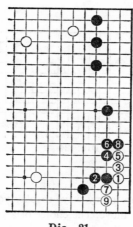

Dia. 21

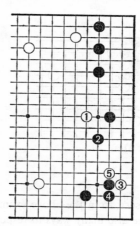

Dia. 22

From the above examples, it can be understood that yosu-miru is a method by which one player tries to determine how to utilize his opponent's bad aji before launching an attack. If the attack is initiated without playing yose-miru, the opponents' bad aji may begin to disappear as we saw in Dia. 7. Here is another example.

Dia. 22

If White plays boshi with 1, Black will respond with 2. Now if White plays tsuke with 3, Black will draw back with 4 forcing White to move toward the outside with the hane of 5. But now the presence of Black 2 will make it very hard for White to play sabaki with 3 and 5 and the chances are that these stones will become very heavy.

So, yosu-miru will either preserve aji, as it does in Dia. 12, or show the way to utilize this aji immediately.

Black 19 in Dia. 2 and White 26 in Dia. 12 are not the only ways of playing yosu-miru against these shimari. The following diagrams give some alternatives.

Dia. 23

Against the ikken shimari, Black can also play nozoki with 1. If White connects with 2, Black gets ko with the sequence to 9. However, please bear in mind that Black should not play this sequence immediately but, instead, keep it in reserve as aji. The procedure in Dia. 3 is now called for.

Dia. 24

If White responds to the nozoki of Black 1 with the osae of 2, Black will play 3. Because of the aji left by the Black stone at 1, White must play 4. Next, Black extends to 5 and the result is similar to Dia. 11.

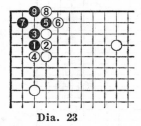

Dia. 23

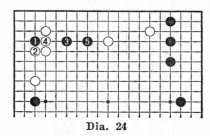

Dia. 24

As seen from the above examples, there are many ways to play yosu-miru. There are also many ways to respond to such a move. The choice of a yosu-miru move or a response may depend on the circumstances but it often depends on the temperament or style of an individual player. It is really impossible to judge whether moves such as these are good or bad. However, there are tactical situations where a yosu-miru type move is the only recourse by which to obtain a satisfactory result. Here is an example.

Dia. 25

White has played tsume with 1 which threatens to invade the Black formation at 'a'. How should Black defend against this move?

Dia. 26

Black should play the sashikomi (insertion) of 2 in response to the tsume of White 1. White must now connect at either 'a' or 'b'.

Dia. 27

In answer to Black 2, if White connects at 3, Black will cut at 4 and after White 5, descend to 6. White must play osae with 7 and now Black can utilize the aji of his stones 4 and 6 by playing 8 with sente forcing White to defend with the kaketsugi of 9. Because of his stone at 8, Black need no longer worry about an invasion at 'a' and can proceed to play another big point.

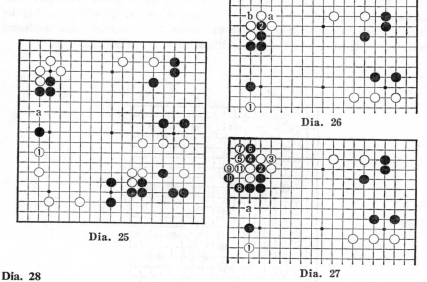

Dia. 26

Dia. 27

Dia. 28

The other possibility is for White to play 3 in response to Black 2. In this case, Black will simply defend his formation by jumping to 4 leaving behind the aji of a cut at 'a'. This aji will be annoying to White when Black invades the upper side. Depending on the circumstances Black may choose to begin this invasion by playing 'b' or 'c'.

Dia. 29

The presence of Black ⬣ makes the invasion of White 1 meaningless. Black plays tsuki-atari with 2 and easily connects underneath with 4.

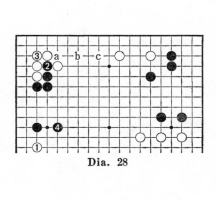

Dia. 28

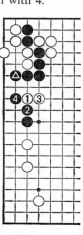

Dia. 29

Dia. 30

If Black plays 1 in response to White ⊘, White will invade with 2 immediately and after Black 3 and 5, it is White who connects underneath with 6, leaving the Black stones drifting without eyes in the center. If Black now plays sashikomi with 'a', White will connect at 'b' and Black has no aji to exploit.

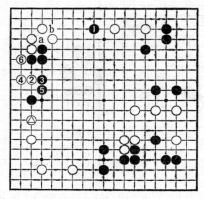

Dia. 30

PART II Problems and Answers

In order to improve one's skill in Go, the first step is to understand the tactical and strategic principles of the game. The next step, and perhaps the most difficult, is to put those principles into practice. This is the experience phase. Playing games is, of course, one way to gain experience in utilizing Go principles. However, without the guidance of a professional teacher, the student often reaches a plateau beyond which it is almost impossible to progress. Fortunately, there is another way to obtain experience; to study problems in which the student can utilize Go principles. The problems in this section all utilize the concepts introduced in Part I and by trying to solve them, the reader can accustom himself to the kind of thinking involved and hopefully apply these concepts to his own games. However, the reader should not be discouraged by failure to solve the problems. The real benefit comes from thinking seriously about each and then compare one's answer with the solution provided. This is the best way to discover and correct your own blind spots.

PROBLEMS

Problem 1   White to play

   After the sequence to White 6, the kaketsugi of Black 7 makes good shape for securing the corner with no bad aji. In any case, it is now White's turn to play. What is the correct continuation?

Problem 2   Black to play

   In response to the osae of Black 4, White cuts with 5, followed by the ate of Black 6 and the sagari of White 7. After this, how should Black continue in order to take complete advantage of this situation?

Problem 3   Black to play

   The sequence in this problem was taken from a four-stone handicap game. In response to the boshi of White 7, Black attaches with 8 followed by the natural exchange of 10 and 11. What should Black do now?

Problem 4   Black to play

   In response to the boshi of White 1, Black plays the keima of 2. The sequence continues with 3, 4 and 5 resulting in a cross cut. There is a proverb which says, "When caught in a cross cut, extend." However, in this case, Black must not follow this rule, but, instead adopt a more aggressive attitude. What is Black's best move?

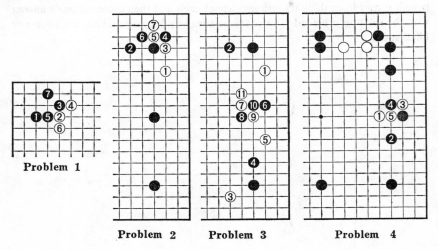

Problem 1   Problem 2   Problem 3   Problem 4

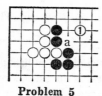

Problem 5

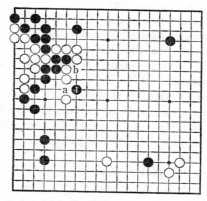

Problem .6

Problem 5 Black to play

White has just played nozoki with 1 aiming to cut at 'a'. Should Black prevent this cut? If not, what is the correct way for Black to play?

Problem 6 White to play

As was seen in Problem 5, moves which seem to be kikashi may not necessarily be so. However, such a move may actually become kikashi if it is obediently answered. In this problem, Black plays nozoki with 1 aiming to push through at 'a'. In addition, White must also consider the effect of a Black cut at 'b'. How should White respond to Black 1?

Problem 7 White to play

Considering the presence of the thick Black wall on the upper side, how should White respond to the nozoki of Black 1?

Problem 8 White to play

This is similar to Problem 7. White must find a good tesuji to make sabaki against the nozoki of Black 1.

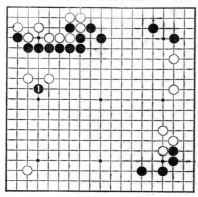

Problem 7   Problem 8

Problem 9   White to play

In order to extricate White ⬡, White initiates the sequence from 1 to 4. After this, how can White make sabaki?

Problem 10   White to play

Black has just played the kosumi of 1, attacking White ⬡. How can White make sabaki?

Problem 11   Black to play

In response to Black 1, White plays boshi with 2 with the aim of utilizing the thickness he has on the upper side. Next, Black plays 3 seeking life on the lower side, against which White plays kosumi-tsuke with 4. How should Black respond to this move?

Problem 12   Black to play

The joseki in the upper left has proceeded to the sagari of White 7. How should Black answer in order to both utilize his shimari in the upper right corner and the aji of his stone at ⬤?

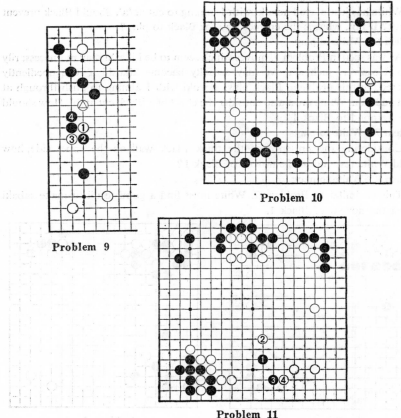

Problem 9

· Problem 10

Problem 11

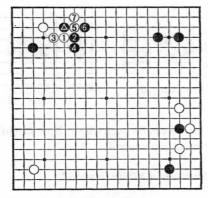

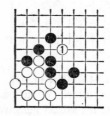

Problem 13

Problem 12

Problem 13 Black to play

White has just played nozoki with 1. Is this move kikashi? How should Black respond?

Reference Diagram 1

The sequence in this diagram is one of the most basic even-game joseki. It is usually referred to as the tsuke-hiki joseki because of the tsuke of Black 3 and the hiki of Black 5.

Reference Diagram 2

In this case, Black has a stone at ⬤ and so, after the tsuke-hiki of Black 1 and 3, White's normal development to White 8 in Reference Dia. 1 is blocked. In this case White 4 is a heavy move and does not make sabaki since there is the possibility of Black playing kikashi with the nozoki at 'a', forcing White to connect at 'b'.

Reference Diagram 3

The correct way for White to handle this situation is to make sabaki with 2 and 4. In order to give the reader a sense of the power of this sabaki, the next few problems will deal with various Black attempts to attack this sabaki shape and other ones similar to it.

Reference Dia. 1

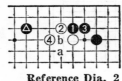

Reference Dia. 2

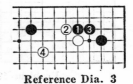

Reference Dia. 3

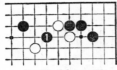

Problem 14

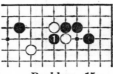

Problem 15

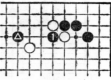

Problem 16

Problem 14 White to play

Black attacks White's stones by jumping in between with 1. How should White complete his sabaki maneuvers started in Reference Dia. 3?

Problem 15 White to play

This time Black cuts with 1. How should White respond?

Problem 16 White to play

In this case, Black ⊘ is one line higher than in Problem 15. How does White make sabaki this time?

Problem 17 Black to play

This problem is related to the preceding three problems. In this fuseki, after the tsuke-hiki of Black 9 and 11, White plays elsewhere. Later, Black comes back and cuts with 15, to which White responds with the nobi of 16. Taking the overall situation into account, how should Black continue?

Reference Dia. 4

The joseki in this diagram was briefly touched on in Chapter 3. After the kosumi of Black 8, it is possible for White to leave the situation as is, waiting to see how Black will attack, with the intention of making sabaki. The next two problems will deal the Black cut at 'a' and the Black hane at 'b'.

Problem 18 White to play

After the cut of Black 1, how can White make sabaki?

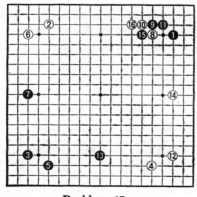

Problem 17

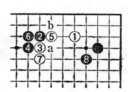

Reference Dia. 4

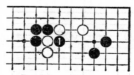

Problem 18

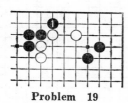

Problem 19

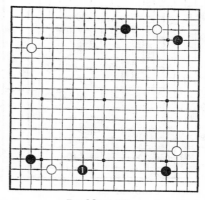

Problem 20

Problem 19 White to play

This time Black plays hane with 1. Again White must make sabaki.

Problem 20 White to play

Black has just played niken-basami with 1. How should White continue?

Problem 21 White to play

After White △, Black plays kosumi-tsuke with 1. How does White make sabaki in this case?

Problem 22 Black to play

There is a rule in Go which advises that when a stone is captured by shicho, it should be removed from the board as soon as possible. In this problem, White has played two joseki on the left side. However, in both of them, White ends by capturing a stone by shicho, at 22 and 30. Because of the bad aji left by this double shicho, Black is able to obtain an advantage in this situation. How can Black do this?

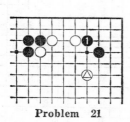

Problem 21

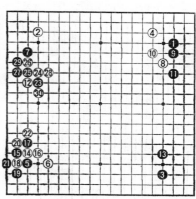

Problem 22

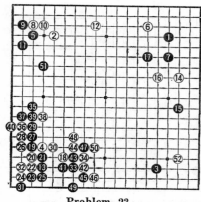

Problem 23

Problem 24

Problem 23   Black to play

This problem is taken from a game between two amateur players. The joseki from White 18 to White 50 is a long and complicated one but well-known to most players. After Black 51, White plays kakari at 52 which is a very big point. However, there is still the bad aji of Black 47 left behind. How should Black take advantage of this aji?

Problem 24   Black to play

Against the kakari of White 1, how should Black answer?

Problem 25   Black to play

In this three-stone handicap game, the sequence to 9 is joseki. In answer to White 9, Black plays ogeima with 10. In this game, White attached with 11 in order to confine Black to the corner. What is Black's correct response from the point of view of yose?

Problem 26   Black to play

White has just played hasami with ⬡ attacking the isolated Black stone on the upper side. When considering this problem, attention must be paid to the weakness

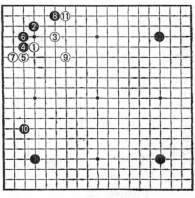

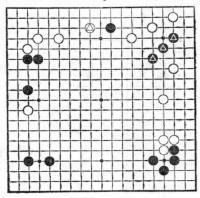

Problem 25

Problem 26

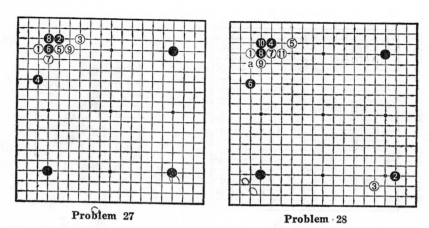

Problem 27   **Problem · 28**

of Black's three stones ⬤. How should Black respond to White △?

Problem 27   Black to play

In response to White 3, Black plays a counter hasami with 4. Once again, White plays tsuke at 5 and the sequence continues as in the joseki studied in Dia. 28 of Chapter 2. However, because of the presence of Black 4, White 9 is not a good move. How should Black take advantage of this mistake?

Problem 28   Black to play

The same joseki takes place in the upper left corner except that this is a two-stone handicap game instead of a three-stone one as before. Please consider the effect of White 3 on the joseki being played in the left corner. Should Black again play the cut at 'a'?

Problem 29   Black to play

In this three-stone handicap fuseki, White attempts to make Black heavy by playing 5 and 7. How can Black make sabaki?

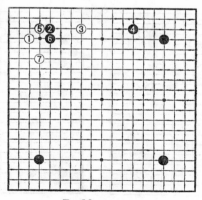

Problem   29

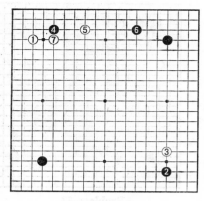

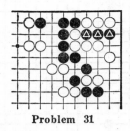

Problem 31

Problem 30

Problem 30   Black to play

This fuseki is similar to the one in Problem 29. However, in this case, it is a two-stone game and White has played tsuke at 7. How should Black answer? Be sure to consider the effect of White 3 in relation to the shicho which can develop in the upper left corner.

Problem 31   Black to play

The Black stones on the upper side are almost dead. However, because of the aji of his three stones at ⬤, Black has a way of saving them. What is the correct tesuji for Black?

Problem 32   White to play

Black plays ogeima at 1, attacking both groups of White stones on the upper side. How should White answer?

Problem 33   Black to play

White has just connected at ⬭. How should Black play now?

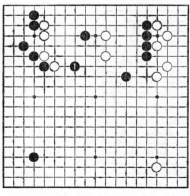

Problem 32

Problem 33

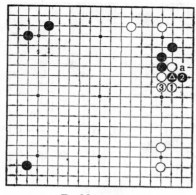

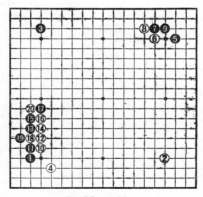

Problem · 34

Problem 35

Problem 34   Black to play

When Black cuts at ●, White 1 and 3 are a standard procedure after which Black must play at 'a'. However, there is a way for Black to play so as to leave bad aji behind for White. What should Black do before playing at 'a'?

Problem 35   Black to play

In Chapter 3, the joseki commencing with White 6 was studied. However, instead of the cut at 16, the osae of 'a' was said to be joseki. Well, what about 16 in this problem? It is really not a good move but White wants to make things very complicated hoping that Black makes a mistake. What is Black's most profitable course of action?

Problem 36   Black to play

This is almost the same as Problem 35 except that White has played 6 and 8. Because of these moves, the shicho which was seen in Answer 35b becomes unfavorable for Black. Hence Black cannot play as before and he must find another way. How should Black continue?

Problem · 36

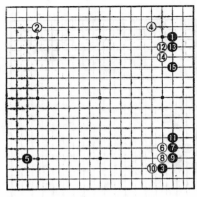

Problem 37   Problem 38

Problem 37   White to play

In this fuseki, after Black plays nobi with 11, White plays 12 and 14. After Black jumps to 15, how should White continue?

Problem 38   Black to play

White's two stones ⬭ are heavy. How should Black attack them?

Problem 39   Black to play

In this four-stone handicap game, Black plays ikken basami with 2 against White's kakari at 1. The sequence continues up to White 7 and it has become very complicated indeed. However, Black can play to turn the situation to his favor. How should he play?

Problem 40   Black to play

Black invades with 1. However, after White 6, Black seems to have been separated from his stones on the upper side of the board.   How can Black play so as to gain the upper hand in this situation?

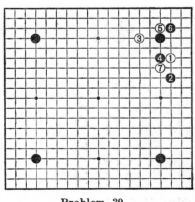

Problem 39

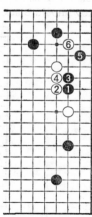

Problem 40

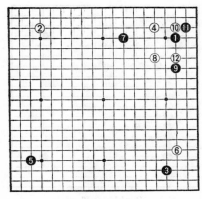

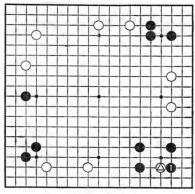

Problem 41   Problem 42

Problem 41   Black to play

White plays 10 and 12 in the upper right corner. In order to avoid suffering a loss, how should Black play?

Problem 42   White to play

Black has played four moves against White ⬡. In spite of this, there is still some aji left. How can White utilize this aji?

Problem 43   White to play

In response to the oshi of 6, Black plays nobi with 7 but this is not a good move. Against 6, what is Black's best response, and how should White continue after Black 7?

Problem 44   Black to play

In this three stone game, the sequence to the cut of White 17 has taken place. What is Black's next move?

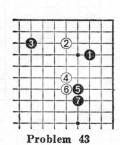

Problem 43

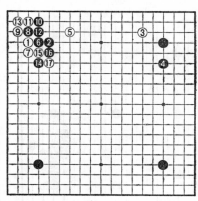

Problem 44

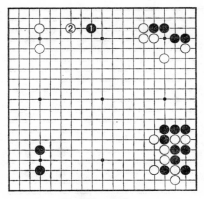

Problem 45   Problem 46

Problem 45   Black to play

In response to the wariuchi of Black 1, White plays tsume with 2. How should Black answer this move?

Problem 46   Black to play

Against the wariuchi of White 1, how should Black respond?

Problem 47   Black to play

This problem is taken from a seven-stone handicap game. Through 16, Black has formed a thick wall while White has made profit in the corner. However, White plays boshi with 17, threatening to nullify the influence of Black's wall. How should Black answer this move?

Problem 48   Black to play

In this four-stone handicap game, Black makes a wall with 10, 12 and 14. Again White strikes at the vital point with the boshi of 15. How should Black respond to this move?

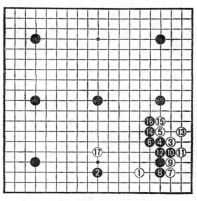

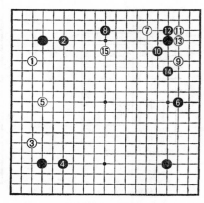

Problem 47   Problem · 48

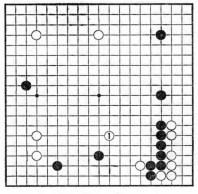

Problem 49

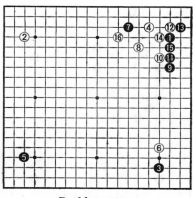

Problem 50

Problem 49   Black to play

How should Black respond to the keima keshi of White 1?

Problem 50   Black to play

In response to White 1, Black plays keima with 2. Next, White tries to make sabaki by attaching at 3. How can Black utilize his thick wall to prevent White from carrying out his plans?

Problem 51   Black to play

In this fuseki, up to 34, White has mapped out a large prospective territory on the right side. However, the kosumi of White 36 is a lukewarm move and not really to the point. How should Black play to make sabaki on the right?

Problem 52   Black to play

White has just played 16. How should Black deal with the upper side?

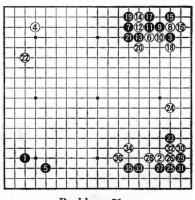

Problem 51

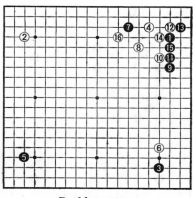

Problem 52

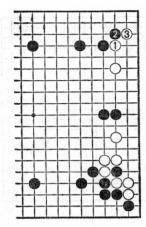

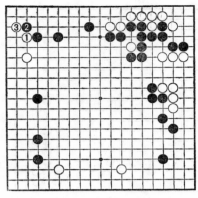

Problem 54

Problem 53

Problem 53 Black to play

White plays ni-dan bane with 1 and 3. Taking the situation on the right side into account, how should Black respond?

Problem 54 Black to play

As in Problem 53, White again plays ni-dan bane with 1 and 3. Should Black respond in the same way as in Problem 53?

Problem 55 Black to play

This problem is taken from a game between Honinbo Shusai, the 21st Honinbo, and Kitani Minoru (now 9-Dan) when he was a young boy. White (played by Shusai) has just made a nozoki with 1. Is this move kikashi, forcing Black to connect at 'a'? If not, how should Black answer this move?

Problem 56 White to play

How should White defend the cutting point at 'a' after the exchange of White ⊚ for Black ⬤?

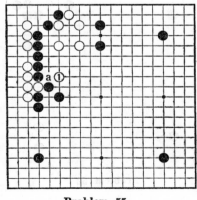

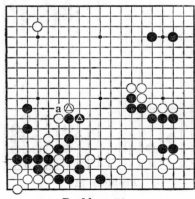

Problem 55

Problem 56

— 74 —

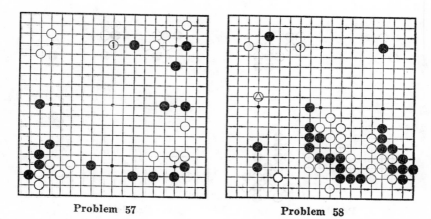

Problem 57

Problem 58

Problem 57　Black to play

How should Black answer the hasami of White 1?

Problem 58　Black to play

Considering the presence of White △, how should Black respond to the hasami of White 1?

Problem 59　Black to play

What is the best way for Black to answer the hane of White 1?

Problem 60　Black to play

Black 1 and White 2 are standard yose moves. At this point, the usual move for Black is the drawback to 'a'. However, because of the presence of Black ●, White's aji is bad. What is Black's next move?

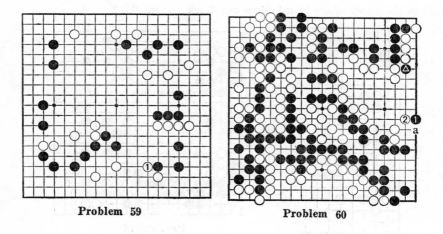

Problem 59

Problem 60

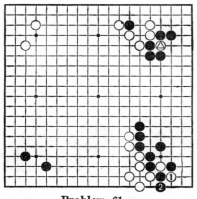

Problem 61   Problem 62

Problem 61   White to play

When Black plays 2 in answer to White 1, it leaves bad aji in the corner. How should White utilize this aji in conjunction with the aji of his stone ⊘ in order to invade the large valley of territory that Black is building up on the right side?

Problem 62   White to play

White responds to the boshi of 1 with the keima of 2, after which Black plays 3 and 5. How can White prevent Black from making sabaki?

Problem 63   Black to play

Black plays yosu-miru with 1. White draws back with 2, Black plays kikashi with 3 followed by the tsuke of 5 and the cross-cut of 7. In answer to 7, White extends to 8. What is the best way for Black to utilize the stones he has just played?

Problem 64   Black to play

White has just played 1, threatening to isolate ⬤ and to form a large potential area in the center of the board. How can Black prevent this?

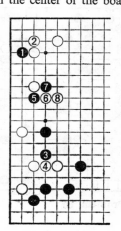

Problem 64

Problem 63   — 76 —

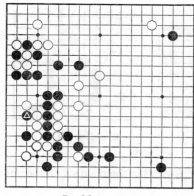

Problem 65

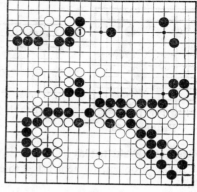

Problem 66

Problem 65 Black to play

How can Black utilize the aji of his stone ⬣ in conjunction with the aji of his stones in the upper left corner?

Problem 66 Black to play

White has just cut with 1. How should Black answer this move?

Problem 67 Black to play

In this five-stone handicap game, White has played at 17, threatening to invade Black's territory on the upper right side. What is the correct way for Black to answer this move?

Problem 68 White to play

This problem is taken from the same game as Problem 67. Before saving his stones on the upper side with 5 and 7, White plays kikashi with 1 and 3. Black now plays nozoki with 8. What is White's answer?

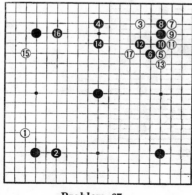

Problem 67

Problem 68

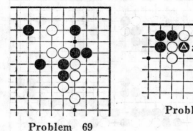

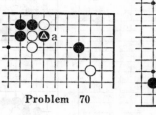

Problem 70

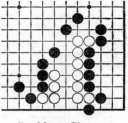

Problem 69

Problem 71

Problem 69   White to play

In this problem, White is asked to escape with his three stones on the upper side.

Problem 70   White to play

White cannot capture Black ● by playing at 'a' because the presence of a Black stone at the 4–4 point renders the shicho unfavorable. However, White can obtain an advantage in this situation. How should he proceed?

Problem 71   White to play

How can White make two eyes for his group of stones?

Problem 72   Black to play

This problem is taken from the first illustrated game presented in Chapter 2. White has just played kosumi with ◯. In the actual game Sakata, Black, launched an attack at 'a'. However before playing here, there is a preliminary move he should make. How should Black play?

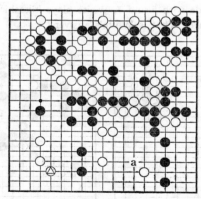

Problem 72

ANSWERS

Answer 1a Correct

The ate of White 1 is kikashi forcing Black to connect with 2. After this, White defends his defect at 'a' with the kaketsugi of 3 making a good shape.

Answer 1b

Eventually, Black may want to play at 1, but now, because of the presence of White ◯, White 2 is sente forcing Black to capture with 3.

Answer 1c

If White neglects to play 1 as in Answer 1a, but instead simply connects at ◯, Black will be able to play 1 and White 2 is no longer sente. Furthermore, Black 'a' may also be possible for some additional points in yose.

Answer 1d

After the connection of Black 2, White must not connect at 3. In response, Black will quietly extend to 4 leaving behind the cutting point at 'a' as bad aji.

Answer 1e

Later on, the nozoki of Black 1 followed by the tobi of 3 is one possible way to attack. This leaves the White stones with a heavy shape. Hence, it is seen that the kaketsugi of White 3 in Answer 1a is essential for making good shape.

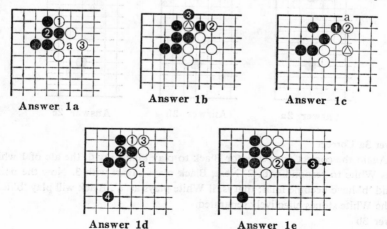

Answer 1a

Answer 1b

Answer 1c

Answer 1d

Answer 1e

Answer 2a Correct

The correct answer is for Black to play kikashi with the ate of 1. When White connects with 2, Black captures two White stones with 3. Let us now consider the effect of Black's kikashi.

Answer 2b

Suppose that Black neglects to play kikashi as in Answer 2a, and instead simply plays osae with 1. In this case, White will play ate with 2 (this is also kikashi) and then play sagari with 4. White's shape is now very good and he can easily make life by playing shibori beginning with the attachment of 'a'. White's shape in Answer 2a, on the other hand, is very heavy and these stones will have problems making two eyes.

Answer 2c

Black 1 and 3 comprise a vulgar tesuji. After White 4, Black must play 5. Next, White plays 6 and his stones will have no difficulty escaping because Black's stones 1, 3 and ● are damezumari. Furthermore, eyes in the corner can easily be made with a tsuke at 'a'. In short, the aji of the two White stones ◯ ensures the safety of White's group on the right side. The kikashi of Black 1 in Answer 1a prevents the utilization of this aji, thereby leaving White with a heavy, insecure group on the right side.

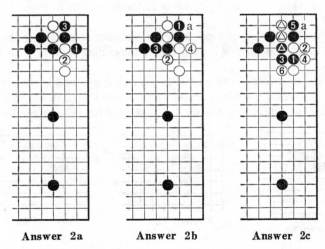

| Answer 2a | Answer 2b | Answer 2c |

Answer 3a Correct

Again the correct answer is for Black to play kikashi with the ate of 1 which forces White to respond with 2. Next, Black plays sagari with 3. Now the points 'a' and 'b' have become miai; that is, if White plays at 'a', Black will play 'b' leaving the White stones effectively separated.

Answer 3b

If Black neglects to play the kikashi of 1 in Answer 3a and, instead, simply descends with 1 as here, White will respond by drawing back with 2. Black has no choice but to jump to 3, after which White plays 4 and 6 to capture two Black stones. The kikashi of Black 1 in Answer 3a can be thought of as a suppression move to prevent this White counterattack.

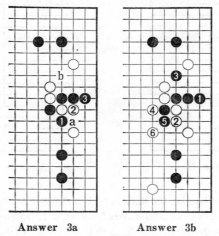

Answer 3a   Answer 3b

Answer 4a Correct

The ate of Black 1, which is kikashi, is the correct answer. After White descends with 2, Black draws back with 3. White must now cut with 4 followed by the ate of 6, but Black utilizes the aji of his stone at 1 to make thickness on the outside with 7 and 9. Furthermore, after Black 9, White needs to play another move to ensure his stones on the right side of life. Now the three White stones on the upper side will come under attack because of the Black thickness.

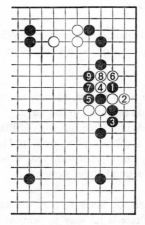

Answer 4a

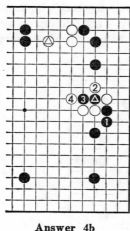

Answer 4b

Answer 4c

Answer 4b

If Black neglects to play the kikashi of 1 in Answer 4a, but instead follows the proverb about the cross cut and draws back with 1, because of the presence of White ⊘, White can capture Black ⬤ in shicho with 2 and 4 .The kikashi of Black 1 in Answer 4a prevents this shicho from materializing.

Answer 4c

The extension of Black 1 in this answer also follows the proverb cited in the problem diagram. In addition, it also prevents the shicho. However, Black is forced to play 3 and 5 in reply to 2 and 4 and, after White 6, Black must defend against White's threatened invasion at 'a' by descending with 7. Next, White will play kakari at 8. Although this way is not exactly bad for Black, the method of Answer 4a is both better and simpler.

Answer 5a Correct

The sagari of Black 1 is the correct answer to White ⊘. If White replies with 2, Black will play kaketsugi at 3 giving his stones good shape while restricting the movement of White ⊘.

Answer 5b

White 1 in Problem 5 aims to cut, so it is natural to consider what would happen if White cuts at 2 in response to the sagari of Black 1. In this case, Black plays 3 and 5. Now, when White plays ate with 6, Black plays shibori with 7 and 9. If White connects with 10, Black plays nobi at 11. White's resulting shape is called "dango" (an eyeless clump of stones) and Black can feel confident in any fighting that may develop around these stones.

Answer 5c

It is out of the question for Black to play the kaketsugi of 1 in response to White ⊘. After White 2 there is no way to prevent White 2 and ⊘ from connecting.

— 82 —

Answer 5d

The connection of Black 1 is also bad since Black's stones become heavy. Black 1 is too submissive, causing White ⊘ to become kikashi.

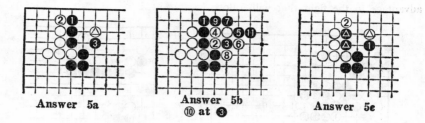

Answer 5a

Answer 5b
⑩ at ❸

Answer 5c

Answer 6a Correct

The jump of White 1 is the correct answer to the nozoki of Black ▲. Because of this move, Black cannot push through at 'a'.

Answer 6b

Against White 1, if Black pushes through with 2, White will block with 3. If Black persists by cutting with 4, White can take advantage of the bad aji of the stones marked ● by playing 5 and 7, forcing Black to respond with 6 and 8. Finally, White captures one stone with 9, leaving the points 'a' and 'b' as miai. That is, if Black cuts at 'a', White plays 'b' which is sente against the Black clump of stones on the left side, followed by White 'c' capturing two stones by geta.

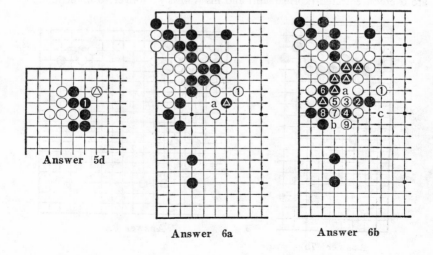

Answer 5d

Answer 6a

Answer 6b

Answer 6c

If White meekly responds to Black ⬣ with the connection of 1, ⬣ becomes kikashi. Next, Black cuts with 2 and the sequence to Black 12 follows naturally. However, White is now separated into two eyeless groups and Black has the advantage in the fight that will follow.

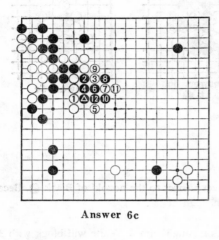

Answer 6c

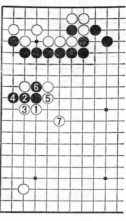

Answer 7a

Answer 7a Correct

The tsuke of White 1 is the correct tesuji. After Black 2, White proceeds to play sabaki ending the sequence with a keima connection at 7. White is left with a good shape radiating throughout the central part of the board, while Black's stones are overconcentrated (korigatachi) and his wall is no longer so influential.

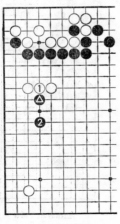

Answer 7b

Answer 8a

Answer 7b

If White connects with 1, ⬣ becomes kikashi and Black will jump lightly to 2. White's three stones are now heavy and, since they fall under the shadow of Black's thick wall, they will be subject to severe attack.

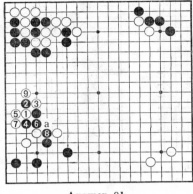

Answer. 8b   Answer. 8c

Answer 8a

It is bad for White to connect with 1 in reply to the nozoki of Black ⬣. This results in Black ⬣ becoming kikashi. Next Black jumps to 2, forcing White to run away with 3. Now Black 4 makes territory along the lower side. In addition to this Black has also formed a potentially large area on the left side of the board. More importantly, White's stones have now become heavy and will make a good target for attack. Hence White 1 must be rejected.

Answer 8b Correct

The attachment of White 1 is the correct answer. The sequence continues to the magari of 7 and Black will be able to form a thick wall with 8. However, with 9, White establishes a position on the left side, at the same time nullifying Black's wall on the upper left. Furthermore, because of the White shimari in the lower right corner and the bad aji in Black's formation at 'a', the resulting Black wall is not so effective.

Answer 8c

Instead of 8 in Answer 8b, what happens if Black plays nobi with 8 as here? White will first play kikashi with 9 forcing Black 10, and now when White connects at 11, Black must play 12. White 13 also forces Black 14 after which White attacks the Black group in the lower left corner with 15. Notice the effect here of the kikashi of White 9. This move gives White one more liberty allowing him to play 11 and 13 with sente which results in furikawari. Moreover White's stones 9 and ⬣ still have some aji left, so Black cannot regard the area on the left side as completely secure. On the other hand, White need not worry about his group since he can easily make life by playing the kosumi-tsuke at 'a'.

— 85 —

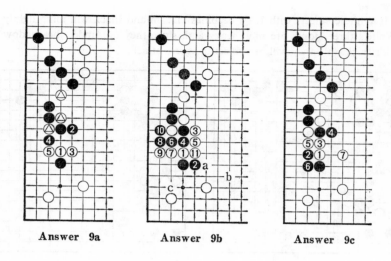

| Answer 9a | Answer 9b | Answer 9c |

Answer 9a Correct

The correct answer is for White to attach with 1 which makes sabaki. If Black responds to this with the tachi of 2, a furikawari sequence results up to White 5. White is satisfied with this result because he has successfully utilized the aji of the three White stones marked ⬭ to obtain a large profit on the lower left side.

Answer 9b

If Black responds directly to the tsuke of 1 with the tachi of 2 as here, White will play kikashi with 3, 5, 7 and 9. After Black captures one stone with 10, White connects with 11 and Black's resulting shape is very bad. For example, if Black tries to escape by playing at 'a', White can attack with 'b', building territory on the lower side at the same time. Also, since White can connect at 'c' at almost any time, his stones on the left side are in no danger. Notice that by connecting at 'c' White leaves no bad aji behind in the lower left corner.

Answer 9c

Another way for Black to respond to the tsuke of White 1 is with the hane of 2. White, however, plays 3, 5 and 7 and this is also bad for Black since his three stones cannot escape.

Answer 9d

It will turn out badly for White if he plays the ate-tsugi of 1 and 3 since Black 4 is very severe.

Answer 9e

It is also bad for White to connect at 1. White 5 and 7 may be kikashi but the resulting White stones are heavy. Furthermore, now that the Black group on the left side is secure, the White shimari in the lower left corner has become quite thin.

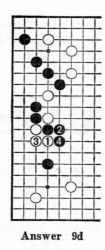

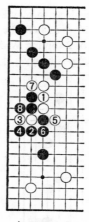

Answer 9d

Answer 9e

Answer 10a Correct

The correct response to Black ⬤ is for White to play tsuke with 1 and, in reply to Black 2, draw back with 3. These moves are kikashi since they evoke a Black response in this part of the board. After Black 4, White can run away with good feeling by jumping to 5 and 7.

Answer 10b

Besides 2 in Answer 10a, Black could also respond to the tsuke of White 1 with the tachi of 2 as here. In this case, White would again play kikashi with 3 and after Black 4, run away with 5 and 7 as before.

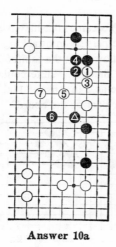

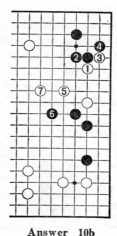

Answer 10a

Answer 10b

Answer 10c

If White neglects to play kikashi as in the preceding two answers and simply plays keima with 1 as here, he cannot make sabaki. In response, Black will play the vital point of 2 forcing White to defend with 3. Next, Black plays nobi with 4 and White's shape is heavy.

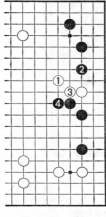

Answer 10c

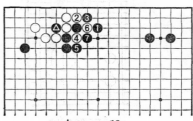

Answer 11a

Answer 11a

If Black simply plays tachi with 1, White will attack with 2. Now Black must try to make life on the lower side or escape out into the center. However, this will be hard to accomplish since Black's shape is heavy. In any event, it can only be done in gote after which White can play at 'a', securing a large area in the center of the board. By playing 1, Black has failed to make sabaki.

Answer 11b Correct

When White answered Black ⬤ with ⬜, ⬤ became kikashi. Now, Black should jump lightly with 1 to make sabaki. If White persists in attacking with 2 and 4, Black will make an eye shape with 3 and 5 followed by the tobi of 7, running out into the center of the board. In response to Black 1, White could play 2 at 7. However, even though this has the same sense as 2 in Answer 11a, Black doesn't have any difficulties making life on the lower part of the board.

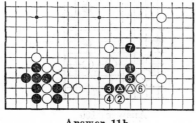

Answer 11b

Answer 12a

— 88 —

Answer 12a Correct

The correct answer is for Black to jump to 1. This move, in conjunction with Black 6 in the problem diagram, makes sabaki for Black. If White continues to resist with 2 and 4, Black can keep White confined because of the aji of ●, with 3, 5 and 7.

Answer 12b

After Black 7, White connects with 8. Now the kake-tsugi of Black 9 is an important move since if White cuts at 'a', then after Black 'b', Black can capture with geta at the point 'c', even though the shicho is not good due to ⊘. In any case, the sequence continues to White 12 and Black will probably connect at 'b' to eliminate the bad aji which remains. As a result, Black has been able to build up a large potential area on the upper side.

Answer 12c

Although the kake-tsugi of Black 1 makes good shape and forces White to respond with 2, it is not recommended here because the distance between this resulting shape and the shimari in the upper right corner is too great. White can aim at the point 'a' and then 'b' when he decides to invade this area.

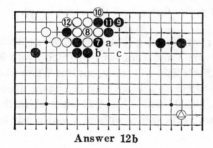

Answer 12b

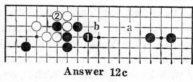

Answer 12c

Answer 13a Correct

The nozoki of White 1 is kikashi and Black must answer by connecting at 2. What would happen if Black chose another response?

Answer 13b

Suppose that in reply to White ⊘, Black plays 1. In this case, White would capture one stone with 2 and, after Black 3, would play nobi with 4 thereby breaking out of Black's confining structure. Well, how about 3 at 4?

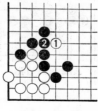

Answer 13a

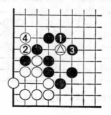

Answer 13b

— 89 —

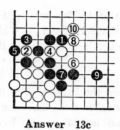

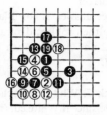

Answer 13c   **Answer 13d**

Answer 13c

For Black to play ate at 3 as here is even worse. The sequence continues to the nobi of 10 and Black has been divided into two weak groups. This is a disaster for Black.

Answer 13d

For reference, this problem comes out of a well-known taka-moku joseki as shown here. In the end, White is able to establish himself securely in the corner while Black's resulting structure radiates power throughout the whole board.

Answer 14a Correct

The correct way for White to play is with the de-giri of 1 and 3. When Black tries to escape with 4, White plays geta with 5 and 7 followed by shibori with 9, 11 and 13. After White jumps to 15, a difficult fight will ensue, but it is White who has the advantage in this struggle. Against 15 and 17, Black must defend the upper side with 16 and 18. Next, White plays kikashi with 19 and 21 after which the nobi of 23 leaves Black's clump of stones in the center without a viable way of playing.

Answer 14b

Since the preceding answer doesn't turn out so well for Black, he ought to choose the simpler move of 2 as here. White continues by playing de-giri with 3 and 5 after which he captures one stone with 7 by shicho. This furikawari is quite satisfactory for White who has successfully made sabaki.

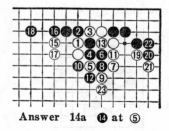

Answer 14a ⑭ at ⑤

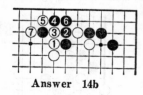

Answer 14b

Answer 14c

Even if the shicho is bad for White, the sequence up to 6 would still be satisfactory.

Answer 14d

But, if because of circumstances, Answer 14c is unsatisfactory for White, White 1 here is another way to make sabaki.

Answer 14e

In any event, it is clearly bad for White to connect with 1 in response to Black ▲. After Black 2, White ⬡ has become isolated and the three White stones are heavy. By responding with 1, White has allowed Black ● to become kikashi.

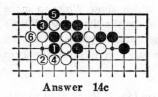

Answer 14c

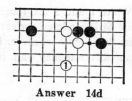

Answer 14d

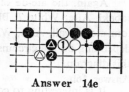

Answer 14e

Answer 15a Correct

One way is for White to play tsuke with 1. After Black plays 2, White descends to 3. As a result, the effect of Black ● is nullified while there is still some eye-making aji left with the White stones at ⬡. The point 'a' seems to be the vital point for White but if Black plays here to prevent White from occupying this point, White will play at 'b' and the aji of his stones at ⬡ comes to life.

Answer 15b Correct

It is also possible for White to play ate with 1. The sequence will continue to the connection of White 7 and now the points 'a' and 'b' have become miai. That is, if Black plays 'a', White will play 'b'. Choosing between this sequence and the one in Answer 15a will depend on the situation on the board.

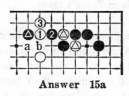

Answer 15a

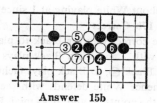

Answer 15b

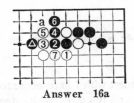

Answer 16a

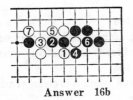

Answer 16b

Answer 16a Correct

Again, the ate-de of White 1 and 3 are tesuji which allow White to make sabaki. After White 7, Black ● is rendered useless under the shadow of White's four stone wall. Also, White 'a' is sente whenever he wants to play it. However, depending on the circumstances, White may want to play 7 at 'a' instead of as in this diagram.

Answer 16b

It is interesting to compare this case with Answer 15b. If Black were to play as in Answer 15b, White could play 7 here with great advantage. This shows a difference between 3rd or 4th line placement of stones.

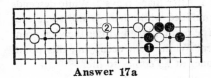

Answer 17a

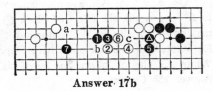

Answer 17b

Answer 17a

Black 1 may seen like a good point but, in reality, it is too slow and allows White to make a good position on the upper side with 2. Besides, Black need not worry about White playing at 1 since the shicho is in Black's favor.

Answer 17b Correct

The correct way for Black to play is with the invasion of 1. White counter-attacks with 2 and when Black plays oshi at 3, White jumps to 4, threatening to capture Black ●, so Black plays tachi with 5. But this move also threatens a play at 'c', hence White defends with the kaketsugi of 6. Finally, Black jumps to 7 leaving the points 'a' and 'b' as miai. Black can make sabaki playing either of these two points. The point to notice here in comparison to Answer 17a is that Black has been able to play both 5 and 7 to make sabaki on the upper side.

Answer 18a Correct

White 1 is the correct answer. Next, Black will play ate with 2 and White must descend with 3. After this, the sequence continues naturally up to White's connection at 9 making Black's corner quite vulnerable. If Black makes shape by extending to 'a' along the right side, White will play at 'b' with sente. Furthermore, White can make eyes in the corner by invading at 'c'.

Answer 18b

For White to attach with 1 is not very good. In response, Black plays kikashi with 2 and 4 followed by an extension to 6 forming a good shape on the right. In this case, White can no longer invade the corner at 'c' as in Answer 18a.

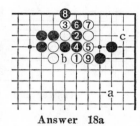

Answer 18a   Answer 18b

Answer 19a Correct

Although it may seem strange, White 1 is the correct tesuji to make sabaki. Now, if Black plays 2, White will ignore it and play elsewhere since he doesn't fear the ate of Black 'a'. In response to 'a', White at 'b' makes sabaki.

Answer 19b

Since Black 2 in Answer 19a is too slow, Black will most likely avoid playing there. Hence, it is quite probable that White will eventually be able to play 1 as here making a perfect eye formation.

Answer 19c

To respond obediently by connecting at 1 is very bad. Black attacks with the nozoki at 2 and White's stones cannot help but become heavy.

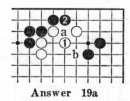

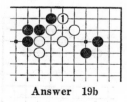

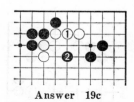

Answer 19a   Answer 19b   Answer 19c

Answer 20a Correct

White begins by playing 1 and 3, followed by the tsuke of 5 and the osae of 7. After Black connects at 8, White jumps to 9. Now Black's position along the lower side is a bit overconcentrated. That is to say, Black's stones 6 and 8 are not working to maximum efficiency.

Answer 20b

Suppose White reverses the order in which he plays the moves in Answer 10a. Now that Black has played his stones at ⬤, he can respond to the kake of 1 with the oshi-giri of 2 and 4. The sequence continues to 8 but now White's stones at 1 and 5 are under a severe attack because of the presence of Black's stones at ⬤.

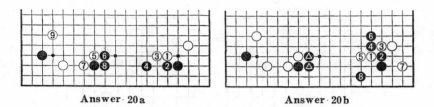

Answer 20a   Answer 20b

Answer 21a Correct

The jump of White 1 is the correct answer. If Black slides to 2, White will make thickness with 3 and 5.

Answer 21b

However, the real value of White 1 lies in the sequence given here. If Black plays hane at 2, White will give up his stone at ⊘ by playing 3, 5 and 7. After Black connects with 8, White will play the kaketsugi of 9 making a good eye shape in the center. Next Black will probably find it necessary to defend his three stones on the upper side, giving White a chance to play kikashi at 'a'.

Answer 21c

The nobi of White 1 is not good. Black ⬤ now takes on the feeling of kikashi. White's resulting shape is now heavy and in some sense without sufficient eyes. White 1 in Answer 21a leaves behind many possibilities and, in that sense, is a very flexible move.

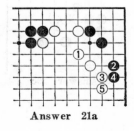

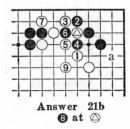

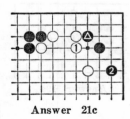

Answer 21a   Answer 21b   Answer 21c

          ⑧ at ⊘

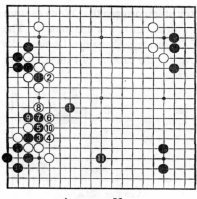

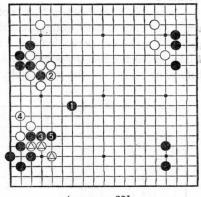

Answer 22a   Answer 22b

Answer 22a Correct

Black 1 is a very skilful move as it threatens to break both shicho. The capture of 2 is probably White's best response but now Black escapes with 3. White 4, 6 and 8 are tesuji but after Black plays 9, White must go back and repair his defective wall at 10. Now, Black takes this opportunity to extend from his shimari with 11. As a result, Black has made profit on the left side while Black's stones at 1 and 11 nullify White's wall.

Answer 22b

If White doesn't like the result in Answer 22a, the other move he can play after Black 3 is the kaketsugi of 4. However, after Black 5, White's three stones ⊘ are in great difficulty.

Answer 23a Correct

Black should play kikashi at 1 followed by 3. This last move forces White to capture Black ● with 4. Next, Black plays 5 and White is in serious trouble on the upper right side.

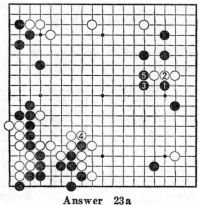

Answer 23a

— 95 —

Answer 23b

Instead of 52 in Problem 25, it is of the utmost importance that White capture with 1. Of course, Black will make a shimari with 2, but this is unavoidable. The point 2 may be very large, but it is a rule of Go strategy that urgent points like 1 take precedence over big points like 2. A move like the capture of 1 must, as said before, be played as soon as possible.

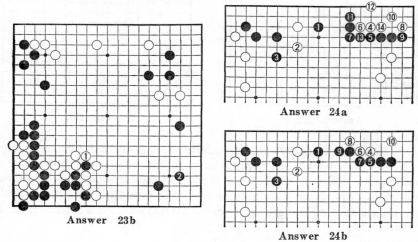

Answer 24a

Answer 24b

Answer 23b

Answer 24a

Clearly, the natural way for Black to play is to make a hasami on the upper side. However, the ikken basami of 1 in this answer, although severe, is not good. The reason is that after the exchange of White 2 for Black 3, there is bad aji in the upper right corner and White can invade with 4, making life with the sequence to 12.

Answer 24b

Instead of 7 in Answer 24a, Black 7 here is also ineffective in preventing White from making life which is accomplished with 8 and 10.

Answer 24c Correct

The correct answer is for Black to play niken basami with 1. Now, after 3, White can no longer make a successful invasion at 'a'.

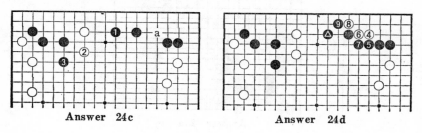

Answer 24c

Answer 24d

Answer 24d

If White should invade with 4, Black will play 5 and 7, but now after the hane of White 8, the osae of Black 9 is possible because of the presence of Black ⬤. This is the move which makes it impossible for White to live.

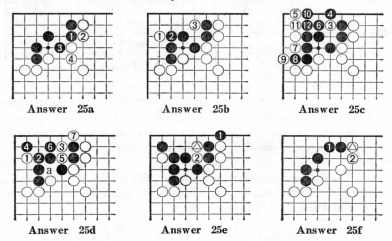

Answer   25a   Answer   25b   Answer   25c

Answer   25d   Answer   25e   Answer   25f

Answer 25a

The tsuki-atari of Black 1 looks like the most logical move, but it is not really so good because after White 4, there is bad aji left in the corner.

Answer 25b

After the sequence in Answer 25a, White will play kikashi with 1 and Black must connect with 2. Next, White plays tsuke with 3. This move is yosu-miru and White's subsequent moves will depend on Black's response.

Answer 25c

If Black responds to 3 with the hane of 4, White will play the sequence from 5 to 11 and Black lives but with gote when he plays at 12.

Answer 25d

On the other hand, if Black plays at 4 in answer to 3, White will play elsewhere leaving the situation as is. When the time is right he can capture two stones with 3 and 5, but this is gote and hence must be postponed until yose.

Answer 25e

It should be noted that the presence of White ◌ prevents Black from making the hane of 1 since now White need only capture two stones with 2. If White ◌ were not present, Black 1 would be a good yose, ending with Black's sente

Answer 25f Correct

Hence, the correct answer to the tsuke of White ◌ is for Black simply to draw back to 1 and if White plays 2, he will end in gote. Consequently, White should not rush to play a move like ◌ and should wait until a bit later in the game.

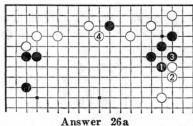 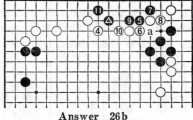

Answer 26a   Answer 26b

Answer 26a Correct

The kosumi-tsuke of Black 1 is the correct answer. White is forced to respond with 2 and Black makes a living shape with 3. To secure these stones in this way is of prime importance. But now White plays kosumi with 4 which seems to take the territory on the upper side. How does Black continue?

Answer 26b

After White 4, Black attaches with 5 followed by the hane of 7. The sequence continues to 11 with Black making life on the upper side. Moreover, White must still worry about the bad aji of the cut at 'a'.

Answer 26c

If Black immediately tries to use the aji of ⬤ and plays 1 and 3, after Black 5, White will play nobi with 6. Now Black's cut at 'a' is useless and furthermore, his three stones on the right side no longer have eye shape. This is an example of using aji too soon. Since it takes White two moves to eliminate the aji of ⬤, Black has time to secure his stones as in Answer 26a. Hence there is no need to rush to save this stone. When utilizing aji, one must be patient.

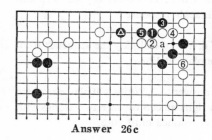 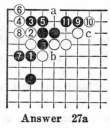 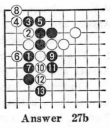

Answer 26c   Answer 27a   Answer 27b

Answer 27a Correct

The correct way for Black to continue is to cut at 1. If White resists with 2, 4 and 6, Black can easily win the fight in the corner because after drawing back with 11, Black can make life by playing at 'a', or by cutting at both 'b' and 'c'.

Answer 27b

After the connection of Black 5, White can live in the corner by playing ate at 6, followed by the sagari of 8. However, Black's stones in the corner can easily escape by playing shicho with 9, 11 and 13.

Answer 27c

It is also impossible for White to capture the Black stones in the corner by playing the sequence in this diagram. Up to Black 25, it turns out badly for White.

Answer 27d

Instead of 9 in the problem diagram, the connection of 9 here is the correct procedure. The sequence up to White 15 is joseki.

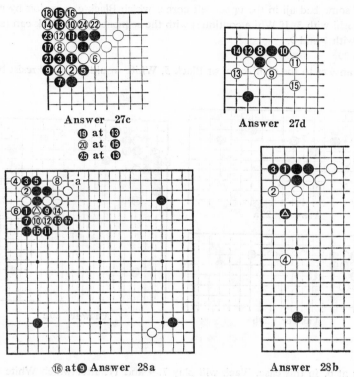

Answer 27c

⑲ at ⑬
⑳ at ⑮
㉕ at ⑬

Answer 27d

⑯ at ❾ Answer 28a

Answer 28b

Answer 28a Correct

In this case, it is still alright for Black to cut at 1. However, after 9, Black cannot capture White ⊘ because the shicho is unfavorable. Consequently, Black plays kake with 11, followed by shibori with 13 and 15, utilizing his five stones in the corner as aji to make a thick wall. Finally, Black plays nobi with 17 and even though the Black stones in the corner seem to be dead, they still have some aji, such as Black 'a' which threatens to revive them.

Answer 28b

Black 1 and 3 may seem like a good way, but now Black ⬤ becomes nullified under the shadow of White's resulting wall and, after White 4, one gets the feeling that it has become a wasted move. In any event, this way of playing is on a very small scale when compared to the way in Answer 28a.

Answer 29a Correct

The keima of Black 1 is the correct answer. If White defends the left side with 2, Black will play kake with 3, severely pressing White's isolated stone on the upper side.

Answer 29b

In response to Black 1, if White defends the upper side by extending to 2, there is some bad aji in the upper left corner which Black can exploit by playing tsuke-koshi with 3. If White continues with the sequence to 8, Black can take the corner with 7 and 9.

Answer 29c

In answer to the sashi-komi of Black 5, White would probably resist by con-

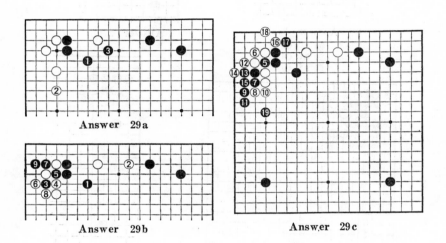

Answer 29a

Answer 29b

Answer 29c

necting at 6. In this case, Black will play 7, 9 and 11, after which White secures the corner with the sequence to 18. Finally, Black makes good shape on the left side by playing 19. Now, White has four stones drifting in the center and Black can be satisfied with this result.

Answer 29d

There is also the tsuke of White 2. In this case, the hane-komi of Black 3 is the proper procedure. If White connects with 6, Black easily makes life with 7 and 9. Besides, White's aji in the corner is still bad and Black can aim to play at 'a'. On the other hand, if White connects at 7 with his move 6, Black will play kikashi at 'b' followed by the tsuke of 'a'.

Answer 29e

It is bad for Black to reply to the tsuke of White 2 with a simple hane at 3. After Black connects at 5, White can defend at 6 and Black's stones are still heavy.

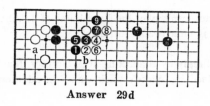

Answer 29d

Answer 29e

Answer 30a Correct

Black should answer with the hane of 1. Because of the presence of ⊘, White must cut with 2. The sequence continues up to White 8 at which time the ate of Black 9 becomes an important kikashi. After this, Black plays 11 and with the sequence up to 17, Black takes the corner while White has thickness. However, Black ▲ nullifies this thickness to some extent so Black should be satisfied with this result. Besides, there is still some aji left in Black's stone at 9.

Answer 30b

In response to Black 9, if White captures ▲ with 10, Black will play 11 and 13, after which he can aim at 'a' to make thickness along the upper side. However, if White plays at 'a', Black will play kikashi at 'b' and then play elsewhere. Now, if White cuts at 'c', Black will sacrifice three stones and make thickness along the upper right side beginning with the ate at 'd'.

Answer 30c

White could also play at 14 in answer to Black 13. This reduces the size of Black's corner area but, after Black captures at 15, White can no longer cut at 'a'.

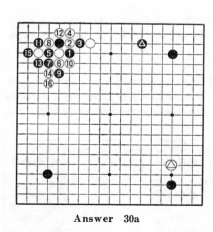

Answer 30a

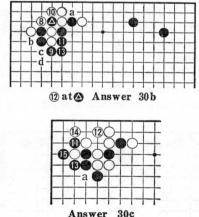

⑫ at ▲   Answer 30b

Answer 30c

Answer 30d

Because of the presence of ◇, Black can't play the hane-komi of 1. After White connects at 4, the shicho at 'a' is unfavorable for Black.

Answer 30e

If Black plays nobi at 1, White will reply by connecting at 2. Up to 9, Black gets the corner but is completely confined by White's thick wall. In addition, White has sente.

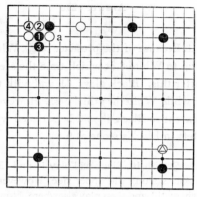

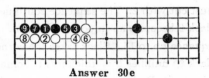

Answer 30e

Answer 30d

Answer 31a Correct

Although it seems to be a suicidal move, Black 1 is the correct answer. This move is kikashi in that it forces White to play at 2. Next Black plays 3 followed by the throw-in of 5 and because of the damezumari caused by Black 1, White can not capture this stone at 'a' but instead must capture with 6. Now Black takes three stones with 7 saving all his stones that were previously endangered.

Answer 31b

It is useless for White to resist by connecting at 2. Black plays 3 and 5. If White continues to try to block Black's escape, he will lose all his stones in the corner after Black plays 11.

Answer 31c

This diagram shows what happens if Black neglects to play 1 as in Answer 31a but instead tries to play ate-komi with 1 immediately as here. White responds with 2 and after Black 3, White captures seven stones on the upper side with 4 and 6.

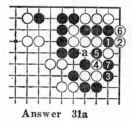

Answer 31a

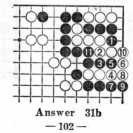

Answer 31b

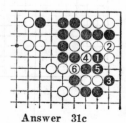

Answer 31c

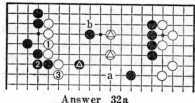

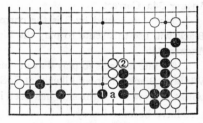

Answer 32a

Answer 32b

Answer 32a Correct

The correct answer to Black ⬤ is for White to connect at 1. Black must now connect at 2 but White escapes into the center with the nobi of 3. Now, White's only problem is to extricate his two stones ⬙ but this is not difficult as he can either run away at 'a' or attach at 'b'.

Answer 32b

In response to White 1, Black cannot play nobi at 2 because there is bad aji in the corner. White will play the tsuke-koshi tesuji of 3 and after the sequence to White 17, Black must fight a ko by playing horikomi at 'a'. This is a bad ko for Black because he has no adequate ko threats.

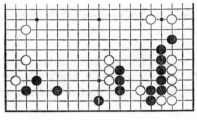

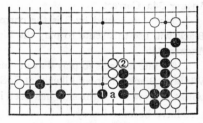

Answer 33a

Answer 33b

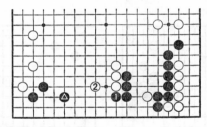

Answer 33c

Answer 33a Correct

In cases such as this, the keima of Black 1 is usually the correct procedure.

Answer 33b

The tobi of Black 1 is not good because after the magari of White 2, there is the bad aji of White 'a' left behind.

Answer 33c

The magari of Black 1 only provokes the tobi of White 2 and Black cannot connect to his stone at ⬙.

Answer 33d

It is not good for Black to play keima with 1. Against this move, White will play 2. Black 3 seems to be the only logical way to continue but after White 4, Black has lost territory on the lower side. Furthermore, the Black area on the lower right side is an example of korigatachi in the sense that too many stones have been invested to take that territory.

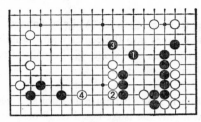

Answer 33d

Answer 34a Correct

Black 1 followed by 3 is the correct answer. If White plays kaketsugi at 4, Black will use this sente to play the big point at 5.

Answer 34b

If White neglects to play 4 as in Answer 34a, and instead plays 4 as here, after White 6, Black will play kikashi at 7. Should White connect at 8, Black will play nobi at 9. Now the right side has been invaded by Black and the five White stones there have become heavy.

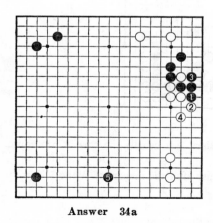

Answer 34a

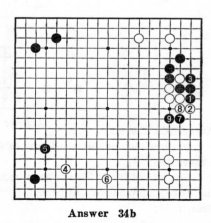

Answer 34b

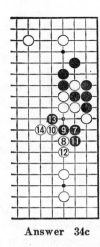

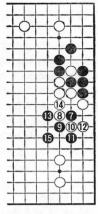

Answer 34c   Answer 34d

Answer 34c

In response to Black 7, White could play katatsuki with 8. However, after 14, White's four stones are still heavy and isolated.

Answer 34d

There is also the tsuke of White 8 in answer to Black 7. In this case, White manages to make at least one eye, but Black has still invaded the right side making sabaki with the sequence to 15.

Answer 34e

Black 1 in Answer 34a is kikashi and it must be played at that time. If Black simply plays 1 as here first and, after White 4, goes back to play at 5, White will respond by lightly jumping to 6, leaving behind none of the bad aji seen in Answers 34b, c or d.

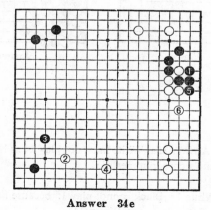

Answer 34e

Answer 35a Correct

In this problem, Black can play ate with 1. After 2 and 4, White plays kikashi with 6 and then crawls along the 2nd line to 12. When Black plays 13, White jumps into the corner with 14. The moves from 15 to 23 are obvious, but 24 is a very good move in that it keeps the fight alive. However, the sequence continues to 31 and Black has managed to escape out to the side. It is now impossible for White to save his stones on the left side by playing at 'a' since Black at 'b' in response will kill them. Hence, White must play 32 in order to save his corner stones. Finally, Black runs away with the keima of 33. The outcome is a disaster for White. It should be noted that it would be bad for Black to play 29 at the point 30 in answer to White 28 since this would result in damezumari and White would be able to save all his stones on the left side.

Answer 35b

When Black plays hane at 25, there is a shicho to consider. After Black 27, White plays kikashi at 28 and the shicho begins with White 32. However, in this case, Black ⚫ works as a shicho breaker so White cannot play in this way.

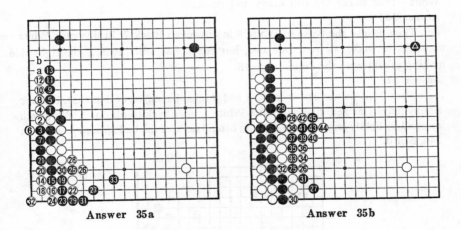

Answer 35a   Answer 35b

Answer 35c

Instead of 24 in Answer 35a, White must not play 24 as here. If he does, Black will play 25 and White's corner stones die.

Answer 35d

In response to White 14, Black cannot play 15 because he will lose the semeai as can be seen from the sequence to White 24.

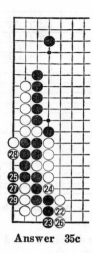

Answer 35c

Answer 35d

Answer 36a

In this case, Black should play kosumi-tsuke with 1. The sequence continues to Black 5 and then White plays 6 and 8. Next, Black plays nobi at 9 and a fight involving these two stones may take place in the center of the board. However, there is bad aji in the White formation with respect to the hasami-tsuke of Black 'a' and this may have an effect on the fighting that could take place in the center. Because of this, the result is not so good for White.

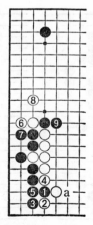

Answer 36a

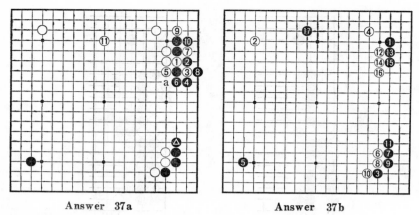

Answer 37a   Answer 37b

Answer 37a Correct

The correct way for White to play is with the de-giri of 1 and 3. When Black plays 4, White will play kikashi with 5, 7 and 9 followed by an extension to 11 on the upper side. As a result, both Black 6 and ⓐ are low on the third line and, consequently, there is some feeling of korigatachi. It seems that Black 6 would be better placed at 'a', but this has been prevented by the kikashi of White 5. Again it is seen how kikashi and korigatachi go hand-in-hand.

Answer 37b

This diagram is taken from the 5th game of the 23rd Honinbo Sen. Black was played by Sakata Eio and White by Rin Kai Ho. After White 14, Black doesn't jump to 15 as in the problem diagram, but, instead plays 15 as here. This move has

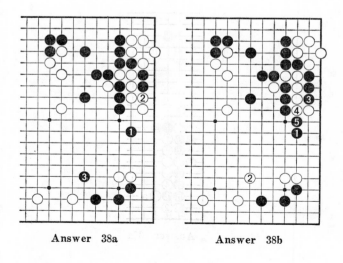

Answer 38a   Answer 38b

the virtue of avoiding both the korigatachi of Answer 37a and allowing Black to leave the upper right corner with sente so that he can play wariuchi with 17 which prevents White from making an ideal extension along the upper side.

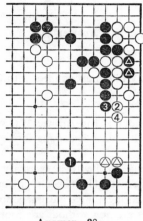

Answer 38c

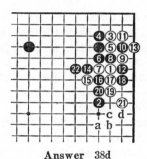

Answer 38d

Answer 38a Correct

Black should begin by playing keima with 1. This forces White to play at 2 and now, when Black plays keima with 3, the two White stones are isolated.

Answer 38b

If White jumps to 2 in answer to Black 1, the aji on the upper right side comes to life with Black 3 and 5 which capture the six White stones on the right side.

Answer 38c

Black 1 in this diagram is a dull move. White is now able to play 2 and 4 which eliminate the bad aji of ⬣ and also rescue his two stones ⬡.

Answer 38d

The formation in the upper right corner is the result of this joseki. This joseki should be studied by all Go players as it contains many examples of Go technique. After White 21, Black's stones at 12 and 18 leave behind bad aji for White. This aji can be utilized by a Black play at 'a', 'b', 'c' or 'd'. However, early in the game it is impossible to tell which point is important so these moves are usually deferred until the middle stage. Problem 38 gives one example of how this aji can be utilized.

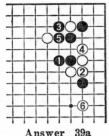

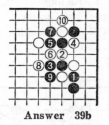

Answer 39b

Answer 39a

Answer 39a Correct

The nobi of Black 1 is the correct move. White must connect with 2 and the sequence up to White 6 results in furikawari.

Answer 39b

If Black cuts at 1 instead of playing the nobi of 1 in Answer 39a, White will play ate with 2 and after the sagari of White 10, Black is completely demolished.

Answer 40a Correct

Black must play the sequence from 1 to 9. White 10 is necessary to make life in the corner and when Black plays hane with 11, it results in furikawari; Black lets White take the corner area while securing a large advantage for himself on the right side. That is to say, White's stones are now without any roots and are drifting aimlessly in the center of the board.

Answer 40b

White 6 in Problem 40 is an unreasonable move. It is joseki for White to play 6 as here after which Black plays 7. In this case, White must be satisfied with his thickness.

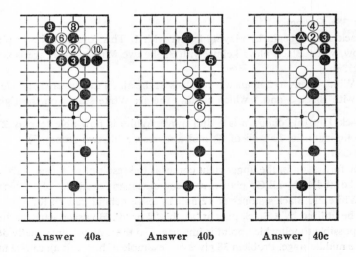

Answer 40a   Answer 40b   Answer 40c

Answer 40c

The oshi of Black 1 and 3 are very bad. After White 4, the value of Black's two stones at ● has been negated.

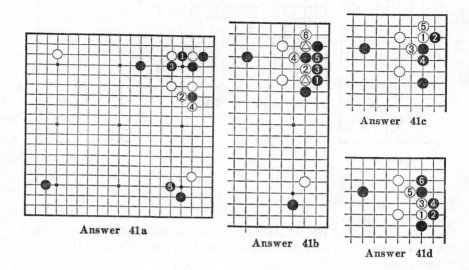

Answer 41a

Answer 41b

Answer 41c

Answer 41d

Answer 41a Correct

Black should play the hane-komi of 1. This will result in furikawari with the sequence to White 4. After this, Black plays kosumi with 5 which has now become the crucial point for both players.

Answer 41b

If Black responds by playing 1, then both of White's ⊘ stones become kikashi. Next, Black will be pressed with the sequence to 6, resulting in good shape for White. Furthermore, Black is pressed into an intolerably low position on the right side.

Answer 41c

The usual way for White to secure his stones is with 1, 3 and 5. In this case, Black can be satisfied with his profit on the right.

Answer 41d

On the other hand, if White plays tsuke at 1, the sequence will continue to the sagari of 6. This time Black gets profit in the corner, and now White's stones at 1 and 3 are damezumari which leaves bad aji behind. If we compare Answers 41c and this Answer with Answer 41b, Black's loss in 41b is easy to understand. Consequently, Black 1 in Answer 41a is the only way to play.

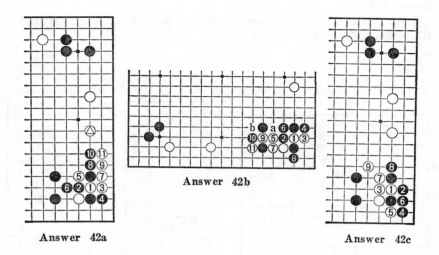

Answer 42b

Answer 42a

Answer 42c

Answer 42a Correct

The hanekomi of White 1 is the correct way to proceed. If Black plays 2 and 4, White will connect with his stone at ⚪ with the sequence up to 11.

Answer 42b

If Black should play osae from the outside with 4 in response to White 3, the sequence up to the cut of 11 will take place. Now, because of the defects in Black's wall at 'a' and 'b', White cannot be prevented from escaping.

Answer 42c

If Black plays ate from underneath with 2, White can escape by the sequence from 3 to 9.

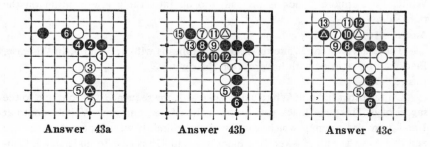

Answer 43a

Answer 43b

Answer 43c

Answer 43a Correct

In answer to Black ⬤, the tsuke of White 1 is the tesuji which initiates the sequence to White 7, resulting in furikawari.

Answer 43b

Black 6 in answer to the oshi of White 5 is bad. Now the aji of ⬙ comes to life when White plays the tsuke of 7. When White connects at 11, Black 12 is absolutely necessary and after White secures himself on the upper side with 15, the opposing groups will fight it out in the center.

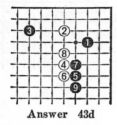

Answer 43d

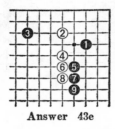

Answer 43e

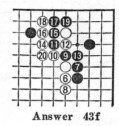

Answer 43f

Answer 43c

In response to the tsuke of White 7, what about the nobi of Black 8? White will play oshi with 9 and after White 13, Black ⬤ has become useless. In addition, White ⬙ still leaves bad aji in the corner. When playing a furikawari sequence, close attention must always be paid to the aji around which the moves focus.

Answer 43d

In response to White 6, Black should draw back with 7 instead of playing the nobi of 7 in the problem diagram. After White plays 8, it would then be possible to play the nobi of 9.

Answer 43e

In order to understand the reasoning in Answer 43d, consider what happens when White plays ikken-tobi with 4. Of course, Black will play the keima of 5, but for White to push Black along the fourth line is very bad since it gives Black too much profit as well as destroying all the aji which exists along the right side. But this is exactly the result in Answer 43d.

Answer 43f

So, when Black draws back with 7, the nobi of White 8 seems to be in the spirit of the situation. However up to 19 Black gains a profit of at least 22 points. White gets a very thick wall but must connect at 20, ending in gote. This is not necessarily bad for White because profit versus thickness is a common result in Go but it always depends on the overall situation. Anyway, Black's profit is very large.

Answer 44a Correct

The best way is for Black to play katatsuki with 1. The sequence up to Black 5 results in furikawari.

Answer 44b

Because of the aji of Black ⬤, it is impossible for White to resist with 2 and 4. Black plays kikashi with 5 and then captures two White stones with the osae of 7. Moreover, Black ⬤ still leaves bad aji behind.

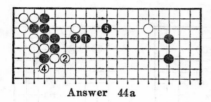

Answer 44a

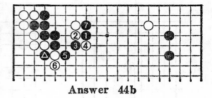

Answer 44b

Answer 45a

The first move that the average player would think of is the extension of Black 1. However, this is a bad move as it breaks one of the basic rules regarding thickness; "Don't approach thickness." Since White's two stones at ⬭ are very strong, Black wants to stay as far away from them as possible.

Answer 45b Correct

There are essentially two correct answers, depending on the style of the individual player; the keima of 1 or the ikken tobi of Black 'a'. Both these moves make an escape route for ⬤.

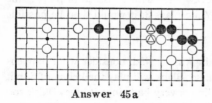

Answer 45a

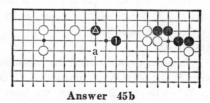

Answer 45b

Answer 46a Correct

Black should play tsume with 1 from this side in order to drive White toward his strong wall. Since Black threatens to extend to 'a', White 2 seems to be imperative. Now Black can continue the attack with the keima of 3. White responds with the keima of 4, following the principle of not approaching thickness too closely. Another virtue of this move is that besides the option of making eyes at 'b', it is also possible to run away at 'c'.

Answer 46b

It is not good for Black to approach White ⊘ from the left with the intention of making territory with his thickness. In such a case, White would calmly secure the lower side wiih the sequence from 2 to 8. Now, when looking at Black's potential area in the center of the board, it is clear that it is not yet real profit but will require at least two more moves to become secure. Trying to make territory out of thickness is an inefficient way of playing. Good Go sense demands that thickness be used for attacking.

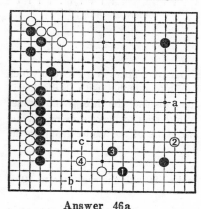

Answer 46a

Answer 46b

Answer 47a Correct

The keima of Black 1 is the correct answer. If White attaches at 2 to make sabaki, Black plays hane at 3 and after drawing back to 5 White cannot play shicho at 'a' because the Black thickness acts as a shicho breaker. As a result, Black has secured the territory on the lower part of the board while White is still drifting in the Black sphere of influence.

Answer 47b

The keima of Black 1 in this diagram is a bad move. Now, since ⊘ has become kikashi, White can make sabaki with the sequence from 2 to 10. In addition, White can play hane-tsugi beginning with 'a' at any time and end in sente leaving Black's stones over concentrated.

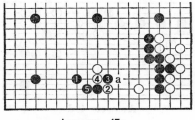

Answer 47a

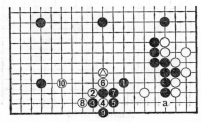

Answer 47b

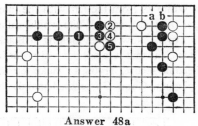

Answer 48a

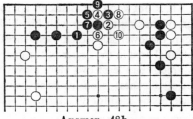

Answer 48b

Answer 48a Correct

The keima of Black 1 is again the correct answer. There is a proverb which says, "Always play keima against boshi." If White attaches with 2, Black will play 3 and 5 utilizing his wall on the right side to isolate the three White stones on the upper side. It should be noted that if White tries to make eyes by playing at 'a', the sagari of Black 'b' has an effect on the life of the White group in the upper right corner.

Answer 48b

Black 3 in answer to 2 allows White to make life with the sequence to 10.

Answer 48c

The keima of Black 1 on this side must be rejected for the same reasons as in Answer 47b. After the tsuke of 2 it is too easy for White to make sabaki on the left. Also, there remains the hane of Black 'a' as aji and Black's shape will be korigatachi.

Answer 48d

When White plays the keima of 2 he aims to attack the Black stones on the right. Consequently, Black must make sabaki with 3 and 5. White is now forced to make good shape with 6 and 8 after which Black secures the upper left corner with 9. Later, Black can descend to 'a' threatening to kill the White stones in the upper right corner by playing at 'b' or to deprive the White group on the upper side of eyes by playing at 'c'.

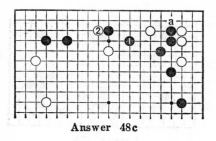

Answer 48c

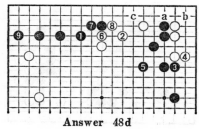

Answer 48d

Answer 49a Correct

The correct answer is for Black to attach at 1. The hane of White 2 is natural, but after the cut of Black 3, White has no really good continuation. When White plays 4, Black extends to 5. Now, in order to defend against the Black ate at 'a', White must extend to 6 and after 7, Black threatens to play at 'b'. It should be noted that with respect to 2 and 3, all shicho favor Black.

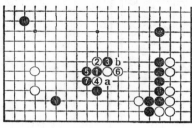

Answer 49a

Answer 49b

If White plays the hane-komi of 2 in response to Black 1, he cannot avoid playing nobi at 6 after Black 3 and 5. Finally, Black connects at 7 and White's stones are heavy and drifting in the center.

Answer 49c

If Black answers with the keima of 1, White ⬙ becomes kikashi. Next, White will play uchikomi at 2 making life with the sequence up to 10. This result is very bad for Black and so he has no choice but to play as in Answer 49a or 49b.

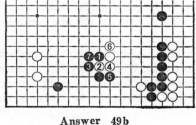

Answer 49b   Answer 49c

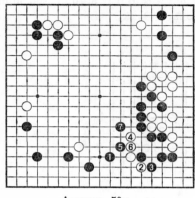

Answer 50a

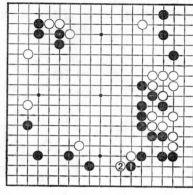

Answer 50b

Answer 50a Correct

The correct answer is for Black to play the keima of 1. This is the vital point for both players. Now there is no way for White to make sabaki or to escape. The sequence to Black 7 shows one variation.

Answer 50b

It is bad for Black to play hane at 1. After 2, there is no way for Black to prevent White from making sabaki.

Answer 50c

If Black plays hane from above with 1, White easily makes sabaki with the sequence to 6. It should be noticed that ⬠ will be of use when White is escaping.

Answer 50d

If Black descends with 1, White ⬠ becomes kikashi and White immediately jumps to 2. Black will not be able to capture these White stones and so Black's wall is rendered useless. The lesson that should be learned from this example is that when one is strong in one part of the board, he should not become embroiled in a fight because his opponent will easily be able to make sabaki. In Answer 50a, Black hit White's vital point of sabaki before he could execute his kikashi. Black, however, was able to do this because of his stable formation in this part of the board which rendered White's subsequent kikashi useless.

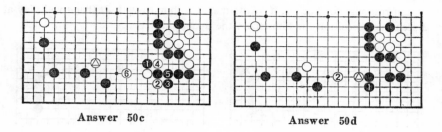

Answer 50c

Answer 50d

Answer 51a Correct

The boshi of Black 1 is just the right point. When White plays keima with 2, Black plays kikashi with 3 forcing White to defend with 4. After Black 5, White's stones on the lower right have become heavy while Black has made sabaki, being able to connect at either 'a' or form eyes by attaching at 'b'.

Answer 51b

The katatsuki of Black 1 is not a very good move. After the sequence to Black 5, White defends his weak point with the kaketsugi of 6 and it is now Black whose stones have become heavy.

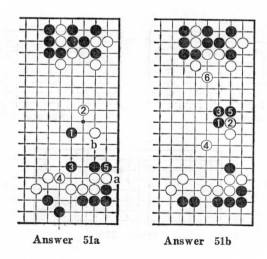

Answer 51a

Answer 51b

Answer 52a   Correct

The correct answer is Black 1. Now the points 'a' and 'b' are miai.

Answer 52b

In response to Black 1, if White makes a shimari with 2, Black will play at 3 securing a position for himself on the upper side

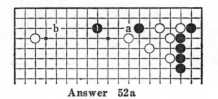

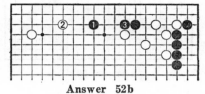

Answer 52a   Answer 52b

Answer 52c

On the other hand, if White blocks with 2, Black will play kakari at 3 and under these circumstances it will be satisfactory for him.

Answer 52d

An immediate kakari with Black 1 is not good since it allows White to play hasami with 2.

Answer 52e

In certain cases, Black 1 is a way to make a light shape. However, here it is not a good move. White plays tsume with 2 and after Black 3, White makes an ideal formation on the upper left side. Furthermore, Black's position still has many weaknesses which can be attacked later.

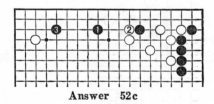

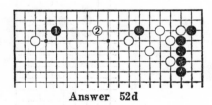

Answer 52c   Answer 52d

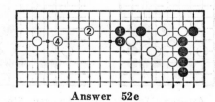

Answer 52e

Answer 53a

Black 1 is joseki, but after White plays at 2, Black's two stones at have become isolated and are heavy. Hence, Black 1 must be rejected.

Answer 53b Correct

In this case, the ate of 1 followed by 3 are Black's best moves. After White cuts at 4, Black continues by securing the right side with 5, 7 and 9. Next, White plays ate with 10 and with the sequence to 17, Black secures almost twenty-five points in the upper right while White gets thickness. However, this thickness is really not so influential in this position.

Answer 53c

Instead of 10 in Answer 53b, it would also be possible for White to take the corner with 10 and 12. However, with 13 Black captures four White stones making an immense outside thickness while White is confined to a small life in the corner. This result is even more unbearable than the one in Answer 53b.

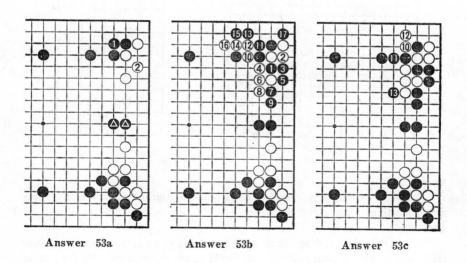

Answer 53a Answer 53b Answer 53c

Answer 54a Correct

Black 1 and 3 are again the correct answer. If the sequence continues up to Black 17, the White wall on the left and the Black wall on the right cancel each other out while Black still retains the corner profit.

Answer 54b

If White decides to take the corner with 4, Black will connect with 5 and after White plays 6, Black has sente as well as an enormous sphere of influence in the center of the board. There can be no doubt that this result is quite favorable for Black.

Answer 54c

Suppose that Black ● is exchanged for White ⊘. Later there is the sequence from White 1 through Black 8. Since White ends with sente, these moves may be considered his option. When we look at the resulting position Black's area on the upper side is small and overconcentrated; in other words, korigatachi. So considering this, the sequence in Answer 54a is the best choice.

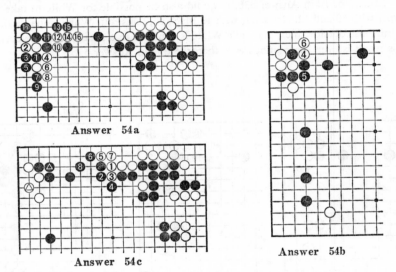

Answer 54a

Answer 54c

Answer 54b

Answer 55a

If Black connects at 1, then White ⊘ becomes kikashi. Next White invades with 2 starting a fight along the upper side.

Answer 55b Correct

In the actual game, Black attached at 1 and this was a very good move. White plays kikashi with 2 after which Black sacrifices his stone at ● with the shibori sequence to 9. Finally, when Black plays 11, White must play 12 ending in gote and Black is left with thickness throughout the center of the board. This result is clearly superior to that of Answer 55a.

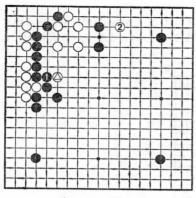

Answer 55a

⑩ connects at ⓐ Answer 55b

Answer 56a Correct

The kake of White 1 is the correct answer and this move makes sabaki. What happens if Black now cuts at 'a'?

Answer 56b

If Black cuts with 2, White will play ate-de with 3, 5 and 7. Next Black plays osae with 8 and White plays shibori with 9 and 11 sacrificing three stones. However after 13, White has made thickness along the left side and the three White stones which have been sacrificed still have some aji.

Answer 56c

In response to White 1, Black might play at 2. In this case, White simply extends to 3. Black 4 is a very important point but against this move, White plays magari with 5 giving White a satisfactory result.

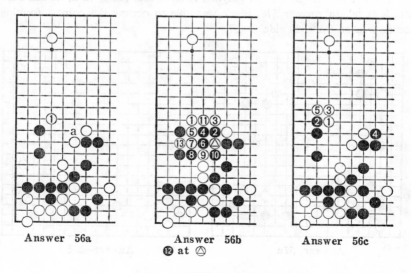

Answer 56a   Answer 56b   Answer 56c

⑫ at ⓐ

Answer 56d

It is too slow for White simply to connect at 1. Not only do the White stones become heavy, but Black can play kakari with 2. This is a dull way for White to play.

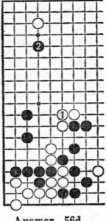

Answer 56d

Answer 57a Correct

The correct way for Black is to jump to 1. White responds with the kosumi of 2 after which Black makes sabaki with 3, 5 and 7. It should also be noticed that Black ⬣ still has some aji.

Answer 57b

Black 1 is a vulgar way of playing. After White jumps to 2, he can aim to attach at 'a'. In Answer 57a, Black was able to occupy the point 2 forming a secure area on the right side.

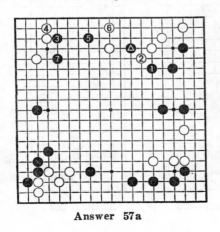

Answer 57a

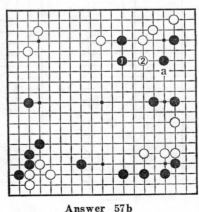

Answer 57b

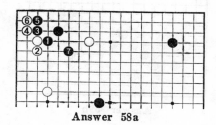

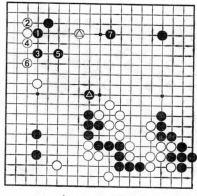

Answer 58a

Answer 58b

Answer 58a Correct

The kosumi-tsuke of Black 1 is the correct answer. If White plays 2, Black stabilizes his stones with the sequence to 5. Should White play 6, Black will jump out with 7 obtaining a satisfactory result.

Answer 58b

Suppose White responds to Black 1 with the sagari of 2. In this case Black will play sabaki with 3, 5 and 7 leaving White ⬡ isolated. Please note how Black ⬢ aids in attacking ⬡. This result is very bad for White.

Answer 58c

The kosumi of Black 1 is not such a good move. In this case, White will play joseki from 2 to 14 after which Black will be in trouble because of the presence of ⬡ on the left side.

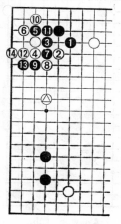

Answer 58c

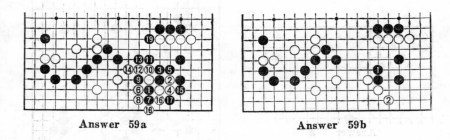

Answer 59a   Answer 59b

Answer 59a Correct

The cross cut of Black 1 is the correct answer. The sequence continues up to White 8 at which time Black cuts with 9 and then plays kikashi with 11, 13, 15 and 17. Finally, Black plays 19 capturing the four White stones on the right side. Furthermore, the shape of White's stones on the lower side is korigatachi.

Answer 59b

The nobi of Black 1 is not good in this case. After White 2, the fighting will shift to the lower right corner and Black will have to make life for his four stones.

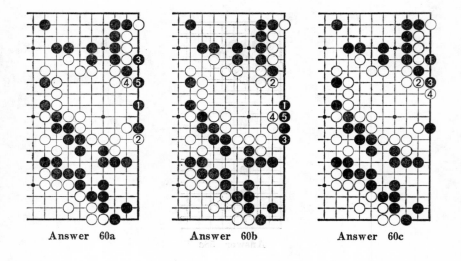

Answer 60a   Answer 60b   Answer 60c

Answer 60a Correct

The correct answer is the jump of Black 1. If White tries to block Black's escape with 2, a ko will result with Black 3 and 5.

Answer 60b

In response to Black 1, White must play 2. However, Black's intrusion becomes even larger than usual after 3 and 5.

Answer 60c

Without Black 1 in Answer 60a, there is no ko. If Black plays 1 and 3 immediately, White will be able to eliminate the aji of the ko by playing at 4.

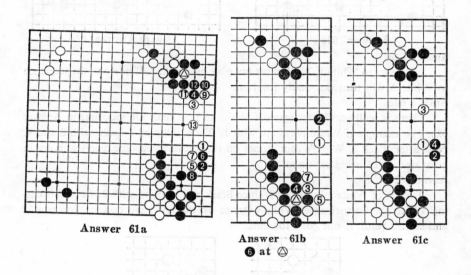

Answer 61a

Answer 61b
6 at △

Answer 61c

Answer 61a Correct

White 1 is just the point since it forces Black to defend the lower right corner with 2. Next White plays kikashi with 5, 7, 9 and 11 finally making sabaki with 13.

Answer 61b

If Black defends the upper side with 2, White will make life in the lower left corner with 3, 5 and 7.

Answer 61c

White 1 on the third line is not good since Black will defend his corner with 2 and after White extends to 3, Black will play at 4 making it difficult for White to form a living group on the right side.

Answer 62a   Answer 62b

Answer 62a Correct

The correct answer is the tsuki-atari of White 1. White will respond to Black 2 with 3 and 5 after which Black 6 becomes necessary. Finally White plays at 7 leaving himself with thickness radiating throughout the center of the board.

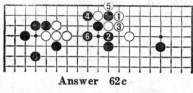   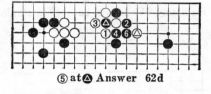

Answer 62c   ⑤ at⊘ Answer 62d

Answer 62b

In answer to White 1, Black must not play osae with 2. If he does, the sequence to White 5 will turn out badly for him.

Answer 62c

There is really no better way for White to play than the sequence in Answer 62a. For example if White plays ate with 1, Black will play kikashi with 2 and 4. Now after Black 6, White's four stones on the left have become heavy and are in great danger of being captured.

Answer 62d

The ate of White 1 is also bad, since Black will respond with 2, 4 and 6 isolating White ⊘. Furthermore, White's stones on the left have become korigatachi and so this result is not good for him.

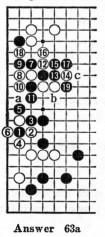   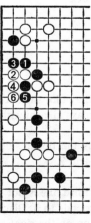

Answer 63a   Answer 63b

Answer 63a Correct

First of all, Black must play kikashi with 1, 3 and 5 followed by 7, 9 and 11. Now because of the presence of the black stones at 3 and 5, White cannot play at 'a' but instead must cut with 12. The sequence continues to White 16, but after Black 17, White has no choice but to play 18. After 19, the points 'b' and 'c' are miai.

Answer 63b

If Black does not play kikashi with 1, 3 and 5 as in Answer 63a but instead plays 1 and 3 in this diagram immediately, White can play at 6 in response to Black 5 and now all of Black's stones on the left side are drifting aimlessly.

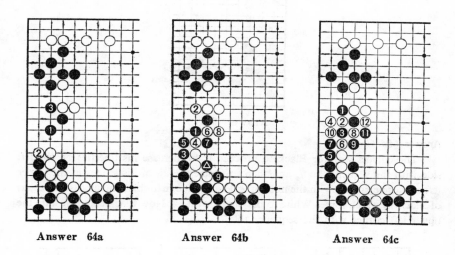

Answer 64a   Answer 64b   Answer 64c

Answer 64a Correct

The kosumi of Black 1 is the correct answer. White must respond by blocking with 2 allowing Black to connect to his group on the upper left side with the hane of 3.

Answer 64b

If White tries to keep Black separated by descending with 2, the aji of Black ⬤ will come into play. Black will connect underneath with 3 and 5. If White continues to resist with 4 and 6, Black will capture five White stones with 7 and 9.

Answer 64c

It is bad for Black to play the hane of 1 immediately. White cuts with 2 and after the exchange of Black 3 and White 4, the sequence of Answer 64b no longer works as can be seen here.

Answer 64d

The sagari of Black 1 is a crude way of playing. Although Black can connect his stones to the group in the lower left corner, his stones on the upper side are seriously weakened after the kosumi of White 8.

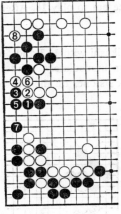

Answer 64d

Answer 65a Correct

The correct way for Black to proceed is to increase his liberties on the left side with the sequence to 7, and then to utilize the aji of his stones in the upper left corner beginning with the nobi of 9. The key move in this sequence is the sagari of Black 13 which forces White to play hane with 14. Now Black can devastate the upper left corner with the sequence to 17.

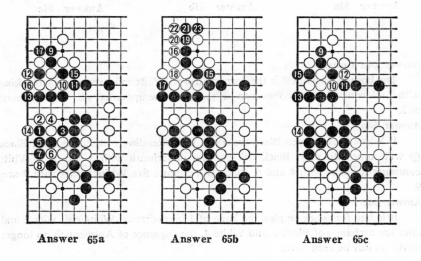

| Answer 65a | Answer 65b | Answer 65c |

Answer 65b

If White plays 16 in response to 15, Black will follow the sequence to 21. Since White cannot fight a ko in the corner, he must play 22 and after Black 23, the result is very bad for White.

Answer 65c

Under these circumstances, White 12 may be the best move. However, White's corner is again invaded with the sequence up to Black 15.

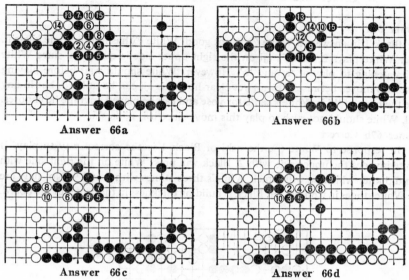

Answer 66a

Answer 66b

Answer 66c

Answer 66d

Answer 66a Correct

The correct way for Black to play is with the ate of 1 and 3 followed by the geta of 5. As can be seen from the sequence to Black 15, it is impossible for White to escape. In addition, the threat of a Black hanekomi at the point 'a' is left behind.

Answer 66b

In response to Black 9, the hane of White 10 also fails. After Black 15, there is no way to save the White stones.

Answer 66c

After the geta of Black 5, White can get furikawari by cutting at 6. With the sequence to 10, Black captures three stones but White also takes three stones on the left side. However, in this case Black has sente and so he can play the hanekomi of 11 capturing a huge area on the right.

Answer 66d

Black 1 is not really very good. After the sequence to Black 9, White cuts with 10 and it is hard to tell how it will turn out. In any case it is not as neat as in the preceding three answers.

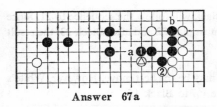

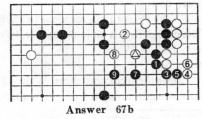

Answer 67a

Answer 67b

Answer 67a

Black 1 in answer to White ⊘ is not good. White ⊘ has now become kikashi. After White plays 2, Black's aji on the right upper side is quite bad since White is threatening to play at 'a' and 'b'. However, White should wait before playing these two moves because it is not yet clear how this aji can be utilized, but in any case the hane of 'b' is White's sente for yose and can be played anytime he chooses. Still, White should not rush to play this move since it is aji-keshi.

Answer 67b Correct

In response to White ⊘, the oshi of Black 1 is the correct way to play. If White invades the upper side with 2, Black will press White on the right side with 3 and 5 after which he will attack White's three stones with 7 and 9. Not only are the White stones in trouble, but Black is building thickness in the center of the board.

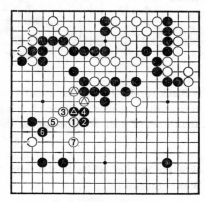

Answer 68a

Answer 68a Correct

The correct procedure for White is to give up his two stones marked ⊘ and make sabaki with the sequence to 7. Black ● is a bad move in that it violates the principle of dealing with kikashi stones; that is, "Do not attack stones which have played kikashi". By violating this rule, Black has allowed White to make sabaki easily.

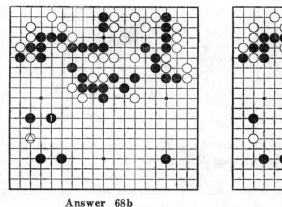

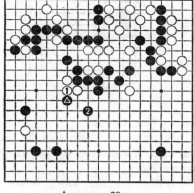

Answer 68b   Answer 68c

Answer 68b

Instead of 8 in Problem 68, Black should have simply played 1 as here. Not only does this move attack the two isolated White stones in the center (from a distance), but it also leaves White ⊘ with less chance to escape.

Answer 68c

It is bad for White to connect with 1. Now Black ⬤ becomes kikashi and White's three stones in the center are heavy. After Black plays 2, it will be very hard for White to escape. Remember the principle: "Do not place importance on stones that have played kikashi". By connecting at 1, White has violated this principle.

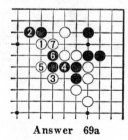

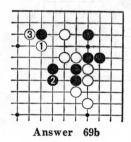

Answer 69a   Answer 69b

Answer 69a   Correct

The attachment of White 1 is tesuji. If Black responds with the nobi of 2, White 1 becomes kikashi and he can capture the Black stones in the center of board with the sequence up to 7.

Answer 69b

Because of the bad result in Answer 69a, Black must respond with the nobi of 2 as here. Next White plays 3 resulting in furikawari.

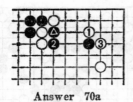

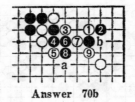

Answer 70a   Answer 70b

Answer 70a   **Correct**

White should attach with the tsuke of 1. If Black rescues his stone at ⬤ by playing at 2, it becomes furikawari when White plays at 3.

Answer 70b

If Black responds with 2, White 1 becomes kikashi and White can proceed to play the sequence up to 9. The points 'a' and 'b' have now become miai.

Answer 70c

If Black answers with 2, White 1 is still kikashi and after the sequence to 10, White again captures the corner.

Answer 70d

It is senseless for White to try to play 1, 3 and 5 without first attaching with 1 as in Answer 70a. This way of playing indicates that White has no plan.

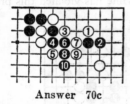

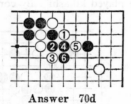

Answer 70c   Answer 70d

Answer 71a

The sequence from 1 to 4 shows that there is no simple way for White to make two eyes. So he must look for a more clever way.

Answer 71b   **Correct**

White must cut with 1 against which Black responds with 2. White continues to make aji in the corner with the kikashi of 3, 5 and 7. Black resists with 8 and now White begins to make eyes by descending to 9. In this case, the sequence will continue to White 13, but here Black cannot connect at 'a' because of damezumari which is caused by the aji of the White stones at 5 and 7.

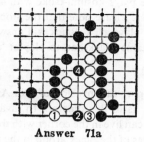

Answer 71a

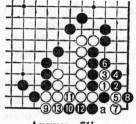

Answer 71b

Answer 71c

So Black must connect with 8, but now White can easily make eyes with 9 and 11.

Answer 71d

In response to White 1, Black might try to resist by playing nobi with 2. However, after Black 4, the attachment of White 5 is tesuji against which Black must play 6. Next White descends with 7 and he can live by the same method applied in Answer 71b.

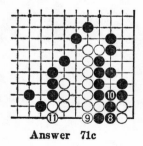

Answer 71c

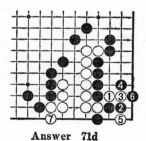

Answer 71d

Answer 72a Correct

Black should invade the corner with 1. This move is kikashi in that it forces White to respond with 2. Now when White plays kosumi-tsuke with 4, the aji of Black's stone at 1 comes to life with Black 5. Please note that the stone at 5 prevents White from connecting since if White plays at 'a' Black will answer with 'b' and White cannot cut at 'c'. In the actual game Black had to play at 'a' and this move had no effect on the White corner.

Answer 72b

There is only one chance for Black to play the invasion of 1 in Answer 72a. If he waits till after White attaches with 2 as in this diagram to invade with 3, White will play hane with 4. Of course Black can live in the corner with the sequence to 9, but White will proceed to destroy the eyes of the Black group in the center with the sequence to 18. To say that Black is in trouble would be an understatement.

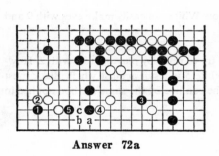

Answer 72a

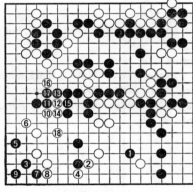

Answer 72b

GLOSSARY

atari a move which occupies the last liberty but one of an enemy stone, thus threatening to capture it.

ate same as atari.

boshi a capping move.

damezumari shortage of liberties.

de a move which pushes between two enemy stones.

fuseki the opening stage of the game, taking the whole board into consideration.

gote to play last in a local encounter; the opposite of sente.

hane a diagonal move played in contact with an enemy stone.

joseki a formalised series of moves usually restricted to the corner.

kaketsugi an open connection.

katatsugi a solid connection.

keima the relationship between two stones which is the same as a knight's move in chess.

kosumi a diagonal move.

nobi extending one stone along a line.

nozoki a peeping move which threatens to cut.

ogeima a large knight's shape.

osae a blocking move which prevents the enemy from extending along a line.

oshi to push along a line on top of a line of enemy stones.

sagari to descend straight down toward the edge of the board.

sente to have the right to choose where to play next; opposite of gote.

shibori squeezing.

shicho a capturing sequence resembling a staircase.

shimari a two stone corner enclosure.

tenuki to play elsewhere, ignoring the opponent's last move.

tsugi a connection.

tsuke an attaching move.

uchikomi an invasion.

wariuchi a wedging move which has room for expansion in either direction.

Bibliography

Elementary books are marked with a single asterisk, intermediate books with a double asterisk and advanced books with a triple asterisk.

All the books listed below are available from the **Ishi Press, Inc.**, CPO Box 2126, Tokyo, Japan or in North America from **Ishi Press International**, 1400 North Shoreline Blvd., Building A7, Mountain View, California 94043. Tel. 415-964-7294. A free catalog of go books and go equipment is available on request.

*G2 Basic Techniques of Go, by Haruyama Isamu 9-dan and Nagahara Yoshiaki 6-dan

A general introduction to tactics, fuseki, endgame and handicap go.

**G6 Strategic Concepts of Go, by Nagahara Yoshiaki 6-dan

Some of the basic concepts of go and the middle game are analyzed, with a large number of problems that utilize these concepts.

ELEMENTARY GO SERIES

*G10 Vol. 1 In the Beginning, by Ishigure Ikuro 9-dan

Required reading for all beginning players. Covers the fundamental ideas of the fuseki (opening).

*G11 Vol. 2 38 Basic Joseki, by Kosugi Kiyoshi 7-dan & James Davies

The ideal introduction to josekis. All the josekis that you need to know until you reach expert level.

*G12 Vol. 3 Tesuji, by James Davies

The basics of tesujis (tactical brilliancies) with over 300 examples and problems.

*G13 Vol. 4 Life and Death, by James Davies

The basics of life and death with over 200 examples and problems.

**G14 Vol. 5 Attack and Defense, by Ishida Akira 9-dan & James Davies

The basic book on the middle game. Covers the fundamentals of positional judgment as well as other topics.

**G15 Vol. 6 The Endgame, by Ogawa Tomoko 4-dan & James Davies

The standard book in English on the endgame. Lots of examples and problems.

*G16 Vol. 7 Handicap Go, by Nagahara & Bozulich

The fundamental principles of handicap go are presented with a problem section.

*G17 Kage's Secret Chronicles of Handicap Go, by Kageyama Toshiro 7-dan

The correct way to play handicap go.

**G19 The Breakthorough to Shodan, by Miyamoto Naoki 9-dan

Basic principles you need to know if you are going to reach expert level. Examples are from handicap games.

DICTIONARY OF BASIC JOSEKI, by Ishida Yoshio 9-dan

***G21 Vol. 1: 3–4 Point Josekis

***G22 Vol. 2: 3–4 & 5–3 Point Josekis

***G23 Vol. 3: 5–4, 4–4 & 3–3 Point Josekis

The standard reference work in English on josekis from the point of view of even games.

***G24 Enclosure Josekis, by Takemiya Masaki 9-dan

Josekis that occur in the middle game with emphasis on the ones that involve attacking and defending corner enclosures.

**G26 The Direction of Play, by Kajiwara Takeo 9-dan

Fuseki theory as expounded by Kajiwara, the great modern fuseki theoretician.

**G27 Kato's Attack & Kill, by Kato Masao 9-dan

Attacking techniques in the middle game. How to attack and kill your opponent's stones.

*G28 Lessons in the Fundamentals of Go, by Kageyama Toshiro 7-dan

A chatty and easy to read book about the fundamental principles of go strategy and tactics.

**G29 Reducing Territorial Frameworks, by Fujisawa Shuko 9-dan

An excellent book on the middle game. All about building and and reducing large frameworks of territory.

G30 An Introduction to Go, by James Davies & Richard Bozulich

*G31 The Second Book of Go, by Richard Bozulich

Written for players who have just learned the rules of go. It covers every phase of the game and aims to set the novice on the right track with respect to the strategic principles of go.

**G32 The Power of the Star-Point, by Takagawa Shukaku

A thorough analysis of the sanren-sei opening pattern.

**G33 The Chinese-Style Opening, by Kato Masao

A thorough analysis of the Chinese-style opening pattern.

Invincible: The Games of Shusaku, edited by John Power.

160 games with detailed commentaries by modern professionals of the greatest go genius who ever lived. A panorama of 19th century go in Japan, the golden age of go. The finest go book ever writen. A must for every serious go player.

The Treasure Chest Enigma, by Nakayama Noriyuki 5-dan.

A entertaining collection of essays about go and its players. The second part is a collection of unique and fascinating full-board problems that is sure to entertain both beginner and advanced players.

*Graded Go Problems for Beginners, Volumes 1 to 4, by Kano Yoshinori 9-dan.

A collection of nearly 1500 hundred problems for the beginner, drilling them in the basic tactics of go.

Go World, a quarterly magazine on go.

The authoritative go magazine in English, published since 1977. All major Japanese tournament games are presented with detailed commentaries as well as general interest articles, go news from around the world, essays and instructional articles.